The Ultimate Herb Gardener

The Ultimate Herb Gardener

Barbara Segall

WARD LOCK

A Ward Lock Book
Cassell
Wellington House, 125 Strand
London WC2R 0BB
www.cassell.co.uk

A Cassell Imprint

Distributed in the United States
by Sterling Publishing Co. Inc.
387 Park Avenue South
New York NY 10016–8810

Distributed in Canada
by Cavendish Books Inc.
Unit 23, Derwent Way
Delta, B.C., Canada V3M 6W1

British Library Cataloguing-in-Publication Data
A catalogue record for this book is available from the British Library

ISBN 0-7063-7690-0

Designed and typeset by Peter Butler
Designs by Gisela Mirwis
Illustrations by Anny Evason and Kevin Maddison
Artwork on page 134 by Wendy Bramall, designed by Tim Newbury

Colour reproduction by Reed Digital, Ipswich, Suffolk
Printed and bound in Italy by New Interlitho

Contents

Introduction

When you are invited to write a book with a wide-ranging yet specific title such as *The Ultimate Herb Gardener,* you discover that it is necessary to move into the realms of the different and the extraordinary. When the subject is herbs, which are among the most valued and useful of all plants, this is not a difficult task. But, just as the title of the book can be read in more than one way, it is possible to adopt both a wide and a narrow definition of the word 'herb'.

Our ancestors knew plants collectively as herbs, and they were as likely to discover, mostly through trial and error, what was safe to eat or to use medicinally and what they should avoid. They regarded herbs as powerful and beautiful plants, which became part of successive traditions, reflected in the folklore and history that is associated with them. The division of herbs into types of plants – trees, shrubs and herbaceous plants – only came later, once gardening had become a decorative art and an established leisure-time activity. Over time, plants that were useful in cooking or efficacious in the pharmacy or useful in cosmetic preparations became separated from other plants and were grouped together in their own specific areas, herb gardens.

Today most of us are inclined to receive medical treatment from conventional doctors or from qualified medical herbalists. This sets herbs free to be used in different areas of the garden. We can still enjoy them for their practical uses, but their ornamental qualities play just as important a role in our gardens as their culinary and medicinal attributes did in the past.

Today, we can pick and choose from a wide range of herbs, and we can grow them in specific herb gardens or use them throughout the garden. We can take our inspiration from the past as well as the present, and the herb garden enthusiast can use herbs formally or informally, to recreate historic periods and places, to tell a story or to explore a theme.

Growing herbs is a multi-sensory experience. There are visual pleasures, as well as edible, tactile and aromatic ones. Herbs may have a long past full of folklore and tradition, but in the modern garden they are real plants, with personality and ornamental attributes *par excellence,* that we see and use every day.

One of the great pleasure of herb gardening is that it takes place as much in reality as it does in the mind. There may be a plant in the garden, such as fennel, that is there for its various culinary uses, but so showy is fennel in leaf and in flower, that it is necessary to hold some of what we know about its appearance and aroma as well as its uses in a sort of 'index-file' in our head. As we brush past the plant and enjoy its fragrance or see its umbelliferous flowerhead dancing with hoverflies on a hot summer's day, we know, understand and see it all at the same time.

The herb garden designs included in Part 2 feature traditional and modern ways of using herbs. Beautifully realized by garden designer Gisela Mirwis, the designs are organized thematically – culinary designs and aromatic and sensory designs, for example, and if you have the space, more than one of these designs can be used within a larger garden. Parts 3 and 4 provide practical advice on building and maintaining the features used in the designs.

Even if you have little space in your garden or if you live in an apartment, you can enjoy the practical and ornamental qualities of herbs. Single herbs on a sunny windowsill will provide material for cooking, and they can be replaced as you use them. On a balcony, in larger containers, you can group together several plants for kitchen use, as well as herbs that you value for their aroma or appearance. Hanging baskets and windowboxes are also suitable for herb growing, although the depth of soil that they hold will limit your choice of herbs.

When you choose plants try to keep in mind how the plants will look at different times of the year and plan to choose from the wonderful selection that is available so that you have variation of texture, colour, shape and fragrance to hold your interest throughout the year.

designing your herb garden

Herb gardens in history

In British horticulture it is known that herbs have been used and grown ever since Roman times. Probably the earliest illustrations showing gardens refer to medieval monastery gardens, however. These were usually rectangular beds, generally holding a single crop, separated from each other by paths and probably demarcated by some form of edging. These small beds could be cultivated easily and, once the crop was harvested, another similar bed was dug and used in the same way. The plants in these basic herb gardens were grown for their culinary, medicinal, cosmetic and sometimes, such as in the case of roses and lilies, for their symbolism in Christian devotion. During the Middle Ages castle gardens developed along similar lines, with plants for culinary and medicinal use being grown in gardens that also provided space for contemplation and renewal.

By the sixteenth century herb gardens were usually attached to universities as well as to many private institutions. The Oxford Physic Garden continues to be a place of research, as does the Chelsea Physic Garden in London, which was founded in 1673 for the apprentices of the Society of Apothecaries. Today, the Chelsea Physic Garden has many modern medicinal beds as well as some of the old ones. One, called the garden of world medicine, displays plants used in China, as well as those used by Native Americans.

Later, the ornamental and functional uses were combined. The earliest parterres, for example, were relatively uncomplicated designs based on box

Geometric shapes are a feature of herb gardens. Chives (*Allium schoenoprasum*) line the square and fill triangles, while box (*Buxus* spp.) and golden marjoram (*Origanum vulgare* 'Aureum') contrast at the heart of the design.

Most herbs are low growing, and an effective way of varying height in the herb garden is to grow one or two, such as this sage (*Salvia officinalis* 'Tricolor'), in containers.

(*Buxus* spp.), with gravel and turf making up the infill area between the highly manicured hedges of box. They gained in popularity in the seventeenth century and gradually became more complicated in design, with plants taking on flowing scrollwork shapes, fluid lines and curves. This style is known as *parterre de broderie*, and once again the patterning was made with box, either with raked gravel or a tracery of turf as the infill. A later variation was known as the *parterre de pièces coupées*, in which box-edged beds were filled with brightly coloured annuals to create a tapestry effect. The style went out of fashion in France with the turmoil of the Revolution, but it was revived and gained in popularity in the nineteenth century, when it was often used in Victorian bedding schemes in Britain.

Once of the first books giving guidance on the subject of cottage gardens was *A Hundred Good Points of Husbandry*, written by Thomas Tusser in 1557. It was a great success and was later renamed *500 Hundred Points*. His view was that the cottage garden was grown by the wife of the small-scale farmer. Tusser's list of recommended herbs was long and included parsley, primroses, salad plants, violets, lavender, tansy, hops, roses, strawberries and sorrel, as well as physic herbs such as mandrake and rhubarb.

Later writers, including John Parkinson in *Paradisi in Sole, Paradisus Terrestris*, which was written in 1629, noted that in the cottage garden of the poor there were all sorts of herbs, including mint, savory and thyme, fruits and vegetables. John Worlidge, writing in 1667 in *Systema Horticulturae*,

Caraway (*Carum carvi*) has attractive, feathery foliage and dainty white flowers, which mature to provide small, aromatic seeds, which are useful in baking.

tells of what he calls 'vulgar flowers', which are likely to have been simply wild or unimproved garden flowers, grown for scent or show, including camomile and foxgloves.

Villandry, a garden in northern France, which was designed in 1906, is a well-known, large-scale ornamental kitchen garden, in which the herbs and vegetables are grown more for their colours and the patterns they make than for their practical use. At Helmingham Hall in Suffolk the large orna-mental kitchen garden balances beauty with kitchen use, but once again the design is on the grand scale.

In herb gardens today, there are still visible links with these early forms, but today's herb enthusiast is fortunate in being able to enjoy herbs as much for their ornamental and aromatic attributes as for their practical value. So while you may choose to grow herbs in a rectangular layout or in a precisely laid-out knot garden, you can also vary the design to suit the site, the overall style of your garden and the way you want to use herbs.

Herbs in the garden

Many people regards herbs as simply the plants we grow for culinary use, such as bay, rosemary and thyme. In fact, the word herb is derived from the Latin word *herba*, which means green plants. All plants are important, fulfilling economic, medicinal, culinary and decorative roles over the centuries, and for the herb gardener there is a wide range to choose from within the usual garden categories of annuals, biennials, perennials, trees and shrubs.

This breadth of choice means that you can plan a herb garden around a group of plants, such as medicinal, culinary or aromatic plants, or you can mix them together and create a garden that holds plants with a variety of uses. Many plants that enjoy a reputation as herbs and that are often included in herb gardens may no longer be practical or safe for us to use in medicinal preparations, but that is no reason to exclude them from your design.

Perennial, evergreen herbs, such as sage, thyme, rosemary and box, will act as all-season ornamentals and provide what designers call the 'bones' of the garden even in the less exuberant seasons of the year. Herbaceous perennials, including chives, fennel and tarragon, will disappear underground during the winter, leaving an empty space above ground. While the foliage of neighbouring plants may cover some of the space, in general you will just have to endure their absence with good grace. Biennials have a two-year growing period, and plants such as parsley, angelica and caraway can help to soften the look of patches of bare ground. Among the hardest working herbs are annuals — borage, pot marigold, summer savory, salad rocket, basil, coriander, chervil, orache and perilla, for example — which will provide the maximum ornament and use in their relatively short growing period.

In spring and summer perennial and biennial herbs can be as decorative as any less useful plant. Fennel (*Foeniculum* spp.), in its green or bronze form, makes a strong, showy stand, growing to about 1 metre (3ft) by early summer and providing a delicate display of small, starry yellow flowers carried in profusion on umbrella-spoked flowerheads. Anise hyssop (*Agastache foeniculum*), which grows to 60–90cm (24–36in) and bears purple spikes of aromatic flowers, combines well with fennel. Angelica (*Angelica archangelica*), which makes leafy growth in its first year and flowers in its second season, is a statuesque border plant. Its yellow-green leaves are attractive, and before the flowers appear the buds make strong fist shapes. The purple form, *Angelica gigas*, adds even more drama to the border. Lovage (*Levisticum officinale*) and cardoon (*Cynara cardunculus*), a silvery leaved relative of the globe artichoke, offer similar height and architectural shape, and both combine well with old roses and everlasting sweet peas, which twine through their stems and across their leaves. In contrast, grey, purple or tri-coloured sage plants (*Salvia* spp.), with their rounded shapes and velvety textured leaves, are attractive for the front of borders and combine well with annuals, herbaceous

Evergreen herbs, including purple sage (*Salvia officinalis* Purpurascens Group), thyme (*Thymus* spp.) and bay (*Laurus nobilis*), will provide year-round interest and form.

plants, shrubs and roses, including some of the most popular modern choices such as *Cerinthe major* 'Purpurascens', which is an annual, and *Guara lindheimieri*, which is a perennial.

Deciding on a style

Whether you grow herbs in a separate area that you refer to as the herb garden, in a themed garden, in a formal or informal bed, or in containers, the beauty of these versatile and useful plants is that they fit into the garden as a whole and can be used simply for their intrinsic ornamental attributes.

In most cases the shape you choose for the herb garden will be determined by the overall shape, style and size of the garden. Geometric shapes were the first choice for the monastic herbers of the past and although it is unlikely that they thought about design in the same way that we might, it was undoubtedly a choice based on ease of access and, therefore, ease of cultivation. Small rectangular beds have been part of traditional herb garden design for centuries, and it should be no surprise that even today they are still popular.

Formal herb gardens are usually geometric or linear, with designs based on squares, triangles or circles being preferred. The formal look is usually achieved by growing neatly clipped hedges or edgings of box or yew at the perimeter of the herb bed. Within the edging the plants may be arranged symmetrically, in geometric shapes, and with a single plant or a piece of statuary as a focal point at the centre. A formal framework can also be provided by growing the plants in a specific design, such as a checkerboard, where groups of plants alternate with paving stones.

The most formal of all herb gardens is the knot garden, a form popular in the sixteenth century and still used today in many large-scale herb gardens. A knot is based on one or two plants that are used as ribbons and planted in curving lines that appear to be woven under and over each other, to create a

Thyme (*Thymus* spp.), purple sage (*Salvia officinalis* Purpurascens Group), common sage (*S. officinalis*), lemon balm (*Melissa officinalis*), bay (*Laurus nobilis*) and golden bay (*Laurus nobilis* 'Aurea') combine around a statuesque chimney in an informal display.

tapestry-like effect. They require patience and time to look their best, and involve a good deal of maintenance to keep the plants well-clipped.

If you have an existing long border, you might want to consider dividing it into a series of smaller compartments – rectangular or triangular – in which you could grow a number of separate, monochromatic gardens. The best way to divide it would be to grow evergreen yew walls, which would act as 'room' dividers. In this way you will be able to create small, but distinct colour gardens.

The same geometric shapes of rectangles, circles and triangles can be used to make informal gardens, in which the herbs are left to grow right to the edge of the bed, without a formal, enclosing edging. Informality is, in fact, the natural choice for most herb gardens, with plants providing the interest through their foliage texture and colour, flower colour and fragrance as well as their overall shapes and heights.

Choosing a theme

The way you intend to use the harvest of your herb garden may provide a central theme around which to plan the design.

A strictly culinary herb garden, planted near the kitchen door, might not be aesthetically pleasing, and it is likely to be so well used that there would be little time for it to be beautiful before you have harvested material from it. It is worth bearing in mind, too, that no matter how well you plan, there is no doubt that herb gardens designed specifically for culinary use, will be at their best at the height of summer, with only the evergreen perennials providing material for use and ornament in autumn and winter.

Culinary gardens can be made more interesting and perhaps provide longer term ornament in the garden if you plan them around the particular herbal signatures of different national cuisines. Popular in recent years is the idea of a 'pizza garden', in which the herbs that provide the essential flavours of Italian cooking are grouped together. Marjoram, basil, bay and rosemary conjure up the flavours of sauces for pasta and of Mediterranean cooking. A garden for English cooking would include parsley, rosemary, sage and thyme, while those with a taste for French cuisine would require sorrel and tarragon, as well as sage, chives and chervil.

Sometimes a herb garden is planted specifically for the intellectual and sensory benefits that many herbs provide. Fragrance from flowers and aroma from foliage act on the senses in a particular way. They can be calming or evoke memories of happy times, and a herb garden based on plants such as lavender, rosemary and thyme, mingled with old roses and lilies, offers a haven of tranquillity, much-needed in a fast-moving modern world. Such gardens also recall the earlier symbolic and contemplative uses of cloister gardens and flowery meads of medieval castles.

Increasingly popular in recent times are herb plantings that have a specific theme. This can be an historic idea, such as a Shakespeare garden, using only herbs and flowers mentioned in Shake-spearean texts, or the design could be based on plants used for medicinal purposes, for wildlife or to provide enjoyment for children.

Colour, too, can be used as the underlying scheme of a herb garden. Ever since Vita Sackville-West created the white border at Sissinghurst, white gardens have been popular and are regularly suggested. White is the absence of colour, and yet can offer an overpowering effect. Such a combination is held together by the foliage, which acts as the foil or anchor.

Hot colours, such as red or yellow, are often chosen to make vibrant, glowing plant combinations. A yellow or golden border can light up a garden, while a red border seems to sizzle and glow like the embers of a fire. Grey foliage and pink-flowered plants are a popular combination, and produce a soft yet interesting effect. Some colours are more retiring and seem to draw the onlooker into the centre of the planting, while others dazzle but keep you at a distance.

Planning your design

Planning for any activity, whether in the garden or not, is the most exciting stage of a project. At this point, the sky is the limit and you can make grand plans or just a few sketched notes. On paper or in your mind you can spare no expense and prepare

the ideal plan. But, as with all activities, eventually reality prevails, and you must adjust your plans to meet the practicalities of your garden.

If you are the fortunate planner of a herb garden, dreams and reality can, sometimes, coexist. The starting point for your plans will be an actual site in the garden. Before you can make any firm plans you have to get to know the site and its conditions. What is the soil like? Is it fertile or will it require thorough preparation to improve the growing conditions? Is the site in full sun or in shade? Is it a wet area or is it exposed to strong winds? For best results, a site in full sun, with shelter from wind is ideal, and you may have to consider whether you need to provide additional protection in the form of fences, walls or hedges of plants, such as box or yew.

A simple sketch is the first stage. It should show the basic shape of the site, with all permanent structures or existing plants marked. Next you need accurate measurements of the site and distances from major features to boundaries or other features. Note down which parts of the site are in shade or sun and whether this varies during the day. Decide whether you will have areas of hard landscaping, such as a paved patio or gravel area, and mark in on your sketches the line of paths – which can be of gravel, stepping-stones or paving. You may wish to place focal features, such as a sundial or a statue, a bench or an arbour, into the design. All these features should be marked on the rough plan, with the measurements of the area they take up clearly indicated.

Once you have all the relevant measurements, decide on a scale, so that the plan can be reduced and drawn onto tracing paper or squared paper. A simple scale is to equate 1cm to 1 metre ($\frac{1}{2}$in to 1 yard). Using this scale, a pencil and a ruler you can draw the plan onto paper and prepare your finished master-plan for the garden. Guidance on marking out your plan on the ground is included in Parts 3 and 4.

Plans are important, but the joy of wayward, spreading herbs is that they may help to create a design that is even more attractive than planned.

Grown together, herbs and vegetables not only make a visually appealing planting but, once harvested, bring fresh tastes and aromatic flavours to your meals.

herb garden designs

decorative
designs

Symmetrical design

Symmetrical shapes have long been popular in herb garden design, and because they can be kept in good order and will generally look tidy, no matter how unruly the herbs may be, they are useful in modern gardens.

The basis of a symmetrical design lies in the geometric or linear shape. The simplest of these is a square, which can be divided into triangles by diagonals running from corner to corner. These diagonals can be marked by, for example, a low-growing hedging plant such as box (*Buxus* spp.), with herbs planted into the four resulting triangles.

You can add to the symmetry by using a standard bay (*Laurus nobilis*), grown to about 1.5m (5ft) high and trained into a mop-head shape, as the central focal plant. Further formality and symmetry can be achieved by embellishing the low hedges. For example, train the plants at the corners or at the meeting points of lines of plants into small globes or pyramids.

The design

Two elements provide the symmetrical formality of a scheme such as this one. The first is found in the choice of edging plant. Box (*Buxus sempervirens*) is used in the design shown here, but yew (*Taxus baccata*), cotton lavender (*Santolina chamaecyparissus*), hyssop (*Hyssopus officinalis*) or euonymous (*Euonymus fortunei* 'Emerald 'n' Gold') can all be kept neat and closely clipped. Their trim lines will hold together the design and the plants within it. The second element is the repetition of blocks of individual herbs.

The well-defined corners of this strong linear design make it suitable for use alongside a path or at the end of a rectangular plot or even as a border between two areas of a garden.

The planting

Box forms the basis of the framework around the planting, creating an edging about 15cm (6in) high and wide. This slow-growing plant will take between three and five years to achieve this size. As

it matures, it will reach a height of 20–30cm (8–12in). The number of individual plants required for such a scheme is high – 140 plants are needed to create this design. The best way to achieve this is to plan ahead and to purchase several large box plants to use as 'mother' plants. Take cuttings from these a year in advance, and by the time you come to put the plan into action you will have the

Edging plants, such as box (*Buxus* spp.), with its small, green leaves, and cotton lavender (*Santolina chamaecyparissus*), with its filigree, grey foliage, will define the design.

Formal French garden

The formal French garden or parterre derives from the knot garden (see page 34). The scale on which these garden styles were once used was symbolic of the importance and status of both the garden and its owner. Both the parterre and the knot garden require a high level of maintenance.

The design was best viewed as a picture and looked at from the vantage point of a raised bank or the first storey of the house. These were not gardens to wander in to enjoy the scent and sight of aromatic herbs. Rather, their stylized beauty was best seen from above and a little way off.

The main reason for the decline in the popularity of such formal gardens was the high level of maintenance needed to keep them at their best, as well as the desire for more romantic, flowing and natural gardens that developed in England in the eighteenth century. Such gardens look stunning planted at the full scale and size, but they are not suitable for the smaller domestic setting unless you use a little ingenuity and imagination and create a formal outline as the basis for exuberant and exotic plants such as lilies and peonies.

The design

The formality derives from the square shape and the infill of a bed of gravel, raked to a perfect finish, as well as from the closely clipped lines of box (*Buxus sempervirens*) that create the outline of the garden. Like the traditional *parterre de broderie* (see page 11), this design has a flowing, sinuous pattern in the centre and curved beds at each corner.

A small knot garden, created with ribbons of colour from dwarf junipers (*Juniperus* spp.), box (*Buxus* spp.) and berberis (*Berberis* spp.), provides a strong focal point and is relatively easy to maintain.

Key to planting

1 *Buxus sempervirens* 'Suffruticosa'
2 *Iris* 'Blue Shimmer'
3 *Paeonia lactiflora* 'Festiva Maxima'
4 *Santolina chamaecyparissus*
5 *Lilium martagon*
5 *Lilium martagon* var. *album*

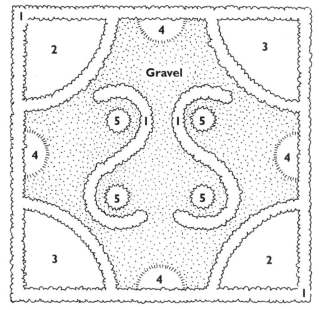

approximately 3 x 3m (10 x 10ft)

The planting

The lines of the square are marked out in box, shaped and clipped to a neat hedge about 25cm (10in) high. The curved beds are also outlined in box, as are the curving shapes of the interior patterning. In between each curved bed and contrasting with the green of the box edging is a soft cushion-shaped planting of cotton lavender (*Santolina chamaecyparissus*), which is trimmed to a round mound, 30–45cm (12–18in) high.

Although the choice of iris (Iris 'Blue Shimmer') and peony (*Paeonia lactiflora* 'Festiva Maxima') for the four beds provides a less formal look, there are strong formal lines in the foliage of the irises and the stately stems of the martagon lilies (*Lilium martagon*) planned for the infill between the scrollwork of box in the centre.

As an alternative to the gravel you could use a creeping thyme (*Thymus serpyllum*) or a non-flowering, creeping form of camomile, such as *Chamaemelum nobile* 'Treneague', to make an aromatic but turf-like infill.

Informal cottage-garden style

The old-fashioned cottage garden, with its informal style, has long been the home of herbs for healing, for cooking and for strewing, as well as for perfuming the house. Usually crammed with as many plants as possible, all jostling for supremacy and flowering and seeding abundantly, the cottage garden has a reputation as a place of exuberance and plenty.

The design
The informality of the cottage-garden style suits small gardens, and the good neighbourliness of the

Informality is the keynote of the cottage-garden style. (Above) plants such as pot marigold (*Calendula officinalis*) and field poppies (*Papaver rhoeas*) mingle without restraint, while (right) a gentle formality is introduced with step-over hedges of apples and roses grown on an iron framework. Sage (*Salvia* spp.), marjoram (*Origanum* spp.), lavender (*Lavandula* spp.) and sweetly scented pinks (*Dianthus* spp.) blend together with a weeping standard rose to give the planting a focal point and variation in height.

Knot garden

The knot garden, the precursor of the formal parterre, dates from the sixteenth century. It was originally a simple, linear design, usually a square or a rectangle, outlined by a plant such as box (*Buxus* spp.) that could be closely clipped to define the edge neatly.

Within the hedging the planting would continue to be geometric, with plants growing together to form intricate, ribbon-like patterns. The ground between the ribbons of grey- or green-foliage plants, such as cotton lavender (*Santolina* spp.) and sage (*Salvia officinalis*), might be filled with gravel, pebbles or even shells. Sometimes the knots were sparsely planted in the infill area with individual specimens of popular plants such as auriculas.

The closely clipped, neat scrollwork of box (*Buxus* spp.) becomes, in effect, a ribbon, holding together the more exuberant flowers planted within its boundaries.

Key to planting

1 *Buxus sempervirens*
  'Suffruticosa'

2 *Buxus sempervirens*
  'Variegata'

3 *Hyssopus officinalis* f.
  albus (white form)

4 *Hyssopus officinalis* f.
  roseus (pink form)

5 *Hyssopus officinalis*
  (blue form)

6 *Salvia blancoana*

7 *Thymus vulgaris*

8 *Origanum vulgare*

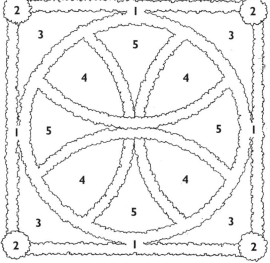

approximately 3 x 3m (10 x 10ft)

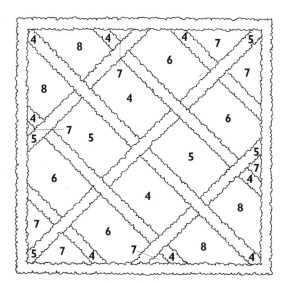

alternative design

Evening primrose (*Oenothera fruticosa*) and cotton lavender (*Santolina chamaecyparissus*) provide contrasting flower shapes in shades of yellow. Together with the dark blue iris, they create an attractive infill between the clipped hedges of box (*Buxus* spp.).

The intricate linking of the plants was reminiscent of embroidery or tapestry work and, like that work, was best viewed from a little way off. As with the formal French garden (page 24), this was from above, usually from an upstairs window or from a raised bank near the knot garden.

The design

Knot garden patterns are often regarded as fairly complicated, but the modern designs shown here are simple yet make effective patterns. The design is based on a circle within a square, with the patterning made by intersecting half-circles. A variation is based on a lattice framework made from different colour forms of hyssop (*Hyssopus officinalis*), with box, the traditional knot garden hedging plant, creating the outline.

The planting

A number of herbs can be used as outline edging plants and for the ribbons of the interior pattern of the lattice design. Cotton lavender, in both its grey-foliage form (*Santolina chamaecyparissus*) and its green-foliage form (*S. rosmarinifolia*), is useful for the inner patterns of a knot garden, and lavender (*Lavandula* spp.) and rosemary (*Rosmarinus officinalis*) are also suitable.

In both of the designs shown here, however, box (*Buxus sempervirens* 'Suffruticosa') is used as the outline plant. Although box is expensive to obtain in quantity, it has the advantages of being easy to maintain in shape and of looking good all year round. It is also long lived and relatively easy to rejuvenate if necessary.

In the circle-within-a-square box has also been used for the inner curves. The colourful and informal infill planting is made up of the three colour forms of hyssop – blue, white and pink. At each corner of the box square outline there is a plant of variegated box (*B. s.* 'Variegata'), shaped into a globe, 45–50cm (18–20in) high, to mirror the curves and circles of the interior pattern.

In the lattice design the inner ribbons are made from blue- and pink-flowered hyssop. The infill plants of this design are different varieties of sage (*Salvia blancoana*), thyme (*Thymus vulgaris*) and oregano (*Origanum vulgare*). Each rectangle holds plants of the same species or variety, so that there is a formal look to the planting.

The box should be trimmed back in spring and summer to keep it looking neat and to maintain the shape, but the only maintenance required for the central, infill plants is to harvest the hyssop flowers and the foliage and flowers from the lattice design to use in pot pourri.

To maintain the flowering plants cut back the hyssops in spring, the thymes after flowering, and the oregano after flowering and again in autumn or spring. Once the sage flowers have set seed, cut back the plants.

Border planting

Herbs are such attractive plants with so many ornamental qualities in their foliage texture, habit of growth, flower colour and fragrance that many favourite garden species – lavender (*Lavandula* spp.), fennel (*Foeniculum vulgare*), pinks (*Dianthus* spp.) and rosemary (*Rosmarinus officinalis*), for example – are as useful in the ornamental border as they are in the specialist or themed herb garden. There are herbs to suit all parts of the border, as well as many shrubs and trees that fit into a general planting.

Herbs such as fennel (*Foeniculum vulgare*), catmint (*Nepeta* spp.) and pinks (*Dianthus* spp.) combine well with perennial border plants.

culinary
designs

Kitchen garden

The most useful and practical of all herb gardens is the kitchen herb garden or potager, where vegetables and herbs grow together in a scheme that combines their culinary use and ornamental value to make the maximum impact.

The large scale of the old-fashioned potager is not usually practicable in the modern domestic kitchen garden, but in a section of the garden measuring approximately 7 × 7m (23 × 23ft) it is possible to grow the herbs that will be of most use for the table, as well as a selection of vegetables that complement them.

The design

The basic square of this design has been divided into several discrete sections separated by small

Ornament and productivity combine in kitchen herb gardens. Box (*Buxus* spp.) can be used to form a neat hedge, which will contrast dramatically with the large, decorative foliage of cabbages.

paved paths so that it is easy to move around the garden without compacting the soil and damaging any of the plants. The paths in this garden are made from brick, which looks attractive. Use engineering bricks, which are frost-proof, and lay them in the same pattern on all the paths to give uniformity and continuity to the design. Cheaper options are gravel and brick-patterned pavers, which will need to be cut to fit the paths.

The central circular area is packed with herbs, some of which are planted in straight lines to form hedges between the larger, wedge-shaped sections of the circle.

The other four irregularly shaped beds in the corners are filled with vegetables. Each of these beds is also edged with vegetables, which make ornamental yet practical hedges.

The planting

In the central bed parsley (*Petroselinum crispum*), garlic (*Allium sativum*), summer savory (*Satureja hortensis*), salad burnet (*Sanguisorba minor*), sorrel (*Rumex acetosa*), caraway (*Carum carvi*), borage (*Borago officinalis*) and dill (*Anethum graveolens*) are planted in straight lines, radiating from the central feature, a sundial. They form informal hedges between the larger, wedge-shaped planting areas of the main circle. Here *Viola tricolor* and *V. odorata*, whose flowers make a pretty and tasty addition to salads, alternate with wedges holding four different species of thyme (*Thymus* spp.), all of which provide piquant flavours for salads and cooking.

Vegetables and herbs are, in general, low growing, so to vary the levels the design includes some plants to provide height. Jerusalem artichoke (*Helianthus tuberosus*), which bears sunflower-like blooms in late autumn, grows to over 2m (6ft 6in) and makes an attractive display before it is time to harvest the tubers from the ground as needed in winter. At right angles to the line of Jerusalem artichokes is a similar row of chicory (*Cichorium intybus*), which can be blanched to use in salads or, in this decorative setting, allowed to go to flower. Its midnight blue flowers (there is also a pink-flowered form) fill the colour gap before the yellow of the late-flowering Jerusalem artichokes.

In the bed on the top left are similar, tall plants, including cardoons (*Cynara cardunculus*). The corners of these two beds are marked with one of the most ornamental members of the brassica family, seakale (*Crambe maritima*), which has a large flowerhead of tiny white flowers.

Each of the four paths in the garden is marked by a pairing of plants. In one, two forms of sage – purple (*Salvia officinalis* Purpurascens Group) and golden (*S. o.* 'Icterina') – make showy mounds, which spill slightly across the paths. Another combines the outstandingly blue-flowered form of rosemary, *Rosmarinus officinalis* 'Severn Sea', with fennel (*Foeniculum vulgare*). The third has angelica (*Angelica archangelica*) and lovage (*Levisticum officinale*), two of the taller herbs, while the fourth combines two plants that need controlling to prevent them from spreading – the variegated form of horseradish (*Armoracia rusticana* 'Variegata') and peppermint (*Mentha × piperita*). Sink them both into individual metal buckets in the ground or into a subterranean container made of slates.

Also adding height to the garden are wigwams holding peas (*Pisum sativum*) and French beans (*Phaseolus vulgaris*). Depending on the style of the garden, the supports can be formal or informal. Hazel poles tied together at the top make informal rustic supports for beans, while hazel twigs make suitable supports for peas. Alternatively, you can use bamboo canes or more stylish wooden tripods.

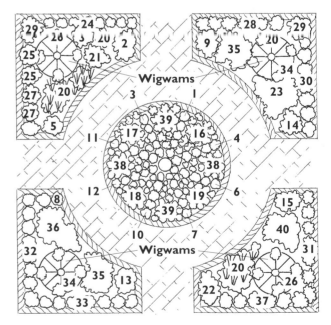

approximately 7.2 x 7.2m (23ft 6in x 23ft 6in)

Key to planting

1 *Petroselinum crispum*
2 *Armoracia rusticana* 'Variegata'
3 *Allium sativum*
4 *Anethum graveolens*
5 *Angelica archangelica*
6 *Borago officinalis*
7 *Carum carvi*
8 *Levisticum officinale*
9 *Mentha* × *piperita*
10 *Rumex acetosa*
11 *Satureja hortensis*
12 *Sanguisorba minor*
13 *Rosmarinus officinalis* 'Severn Sea'

14 *Salvia officinalis* Purpurascens Group
15 *Salvia officinalis* 'Icterina'
16 *Thymus vulgaris* 'Silver Posie'
17 *Thymus serpyllum* 'Pink Chintz'
18 *Thymus* 'Doone Valley'
19 *Thymus* × *citriodorus* 'Bertram Anderson'
20 *Allium tuberosum*
21 *Allium fistulosum*
22 *Foeniculum vulgare*
23 *Rheum* × *hybridum* (syn. *R.* × *cultorum*)

24 *Pastinaca sativa* (parsnip)
25 *Cynara cardunculus*
26 *Phaseolus vulgaris*
27 *Asparagus officinalis*
28 *Cichorium intybus*
29 *Crambe maritima*
30 *Helianthus tuberosus* 'Fuseau'
31 *Lactuca sativa* 'Oak Leaf' and 'Lollo' (lettuce)
32 *Lycospersicon esculentum* 'Sungold' and 'Gardeners' Delight' (tomato)

33 *Raphanus sativus* 'French Breakfast' (radish)
34 *Pisum sativum* 'Sugar Snap'
35 *Tropaeolum majus* 'Alaska'
36 *Eruca vesicaria* subsp. *sativa* (rocket)
37 *Spinacia oleracea* followed by *Beta vulgaris* (spinach)
38 *Viola tricolor*
39 *Viola odorata*
40 *Beta vulgaris* 'Ruby Chard' (Swiss chard)

Backdoor herb garden

These two small beds, arranged in triangular sections to hold as many different species as possible, will provide herbs just outside your backdoor. This is the ideal place to grow the herbs that are most often used in the kitchen, because they will be easy and convenient to harvest. Although the two beds will have immediate and ongoing practical use, they will also have a decorative element to provide visual pleasure as well.

Grow the herbs that you use most often – parsley (*Petroselinum* spp.), sage (*Salvia* spp.) and chives (*Allium schoenoprasum*), for example – in small blocks near the backdoor.

The design

The scheme is a simple yet effective use for the often wasted space beside the backdoor. Separated by the back step, each bed measures roughly 2 × 0.6m (6ft 6in × 2ft) and is backed by the house wall. Some of the herbs growing near to the wall, such as chervil (*Anthriscus cerefolium*), will benefit from the partially shaded situation.

The dividing lines between the various herbs can be formally marked with lines of loosely placed bricks or with a shading of gravel. When you mark out and plant up the beds, it is quite easy to indicate the lines of the triangles with a cane and handfuls of gravel so that you can plant up the sections evenly. Eventually, as the plants grow, the foliage textures and colours and the individual shapes will create their own demarcation lines.

You could divide the beds with straight lines rather than into triangles, but this would mean that in winter the bare sections where perennials, such as chives (*Allium schoenoprasum*), or annuals, such as coriander (*Coriandrum sativum*), are missing would look even more noticeable. Another possible scheme would be to grow the herbs in small squares.

The plants

Chervil and mint (*Mentha spicata* 'Moroccan'), which are planted at the far end of each of the beds, will enjoy some of the partial shade offered by the lee of the wall, as will coriander, especially if it is being grown for its leaves, as long as watering is not neglected. Sow coriander, fennel (*Foeniculum vulgare*) and chervil seed in spring direct into the growing site or buy young plants. It is said that coriander inhibits fennel's ability to produce seed, so you may wish to separate the plants even further than indicated on the plan.

On each side of the backdoor is a section devoted to plants whose aromatic foliage will grow over the edge of the back step and release their fragrance whenever you brush past them. Sage (*Salvia officinalis*) and rosemary (*Rosmarinus officinalis* 'Miss Jessopp's Upright') have been used.

In spring and summer you will be able to pick material from all the plants. Pick evenly from each plant or from different plants on different occasions, so that you maintain the overall balance of the planting. In winter you will have a limited amount of leafy material from plants such as winter savory (*Satureja montana*), sage, rosemary, thyme (*Thymus × citriodorus* 'Bertram Anderson'), marjoram (*Origanum vulgare*) and parsley (*Petroselinum crispum*).

Key to planting
1 *Anthriscus cerefolium*
2 *Coriandrum sativum*
3 *Allium schoenoprasum*
4 *Rosmarinus officinalis* 'Miss Jessopp's Upright'
5 *Thymus × citriodorus* 'Bertram Anderson'
6 *Foeniculum vulgare*
7 *Satureja montana*
8 *Rumex scutatus*
9 *Origanum vulgare*
10 *Myrrhis odorata*
11 *Petroselinum crispum*
12 *Levisticum officinale*
13 *Salvia officinalis*
14 *Mentha spicata* 'Moroccan'
15 *Artemisia dracunculus*

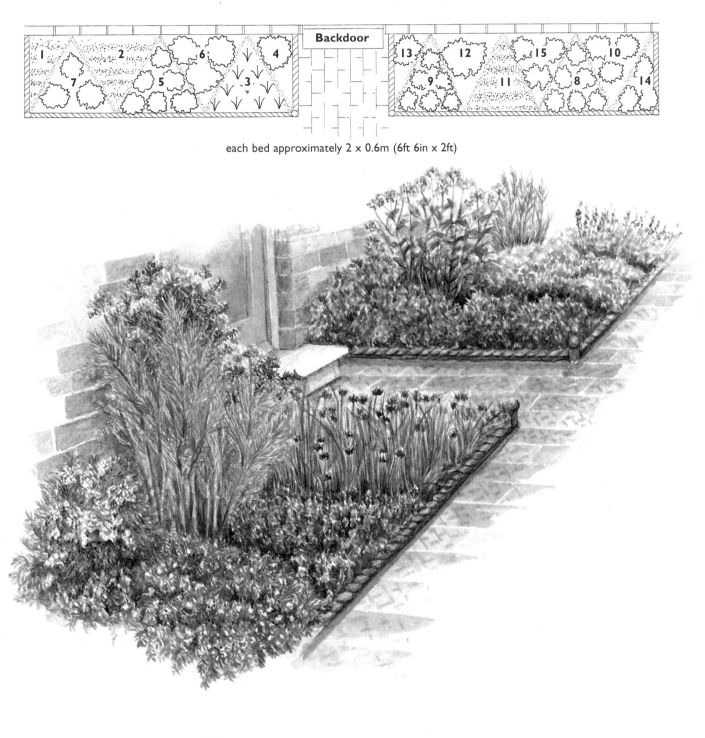

each bed approximately 2 × 0.6m (6ft 6in x 2ft)

One-herb collection

A number of herb genera include species and varieties that vary widely in their leaves and flowers as well as in their aromas. A one-herb collection will enable you to display such herbs in a way that will make these contrasts more visible and dramatic.

Sage (*Salvia* spp.), thyme (*Thymus* spp.), mint (*Mentha* spp.), rosemary (*Rosmarinus* spp.), lavender (*Lavandula* spp.) and basil (*Ocimum* spp.) are all candidates for this treatment. Not all of the species available are necessarily useful for culinary purposes, so it is best to think of the area that will hold them primarily as a display bed. First, read all you can about the genus and the needs of the different species that you want to collect. Once you know how they grow, you can begin to plan the shape of a bed that will display them well and make the differences and the similarities between them dramatically obvious as well as ornamental. Two possible designs are shown here. The first is a sage circle; the variation is a thyme trough.

The design

Because sage plants are, in general, shrubby and bushy, a classic circular planting such as a herb wheel (see page 30) is one of the best ways to show off their foliage. You will need a large circle with a diameter of about 1.8m (6ft) to hold a good-sized collection of sages. Edge the circle and mark the divisions between sections with bricks laid end to end. A similar circle would suit lavender, mint and rosemary.

Sages need well-drained, almost sandy soil in the sunniest site in the garden if they are to perform well. Cover the surface of the soil with gravel after you have finished planting to prevent evaporation from the soil's surface and to help bake the plant's roots, providing the conditions in which they thrive.

The planting

The sages used in this planting vary dramatically in their leaf shape, size and colour, and if they are left to flower they will continue to make an attractive feature in the garden until quite late in the year.

To create a focal point at the centre of the circle, use the tall-growing, candelabra-like clary sage (*Salvia sclarea* var. *turkestanica*). This is not an edible form of the herb, but the pink-tinged,

There are more than 15 different types of basil (*Ocimum* spp.) available. They vary in foliage, shape, colour and flavour, and they make an attractive group in containers or in the garden.

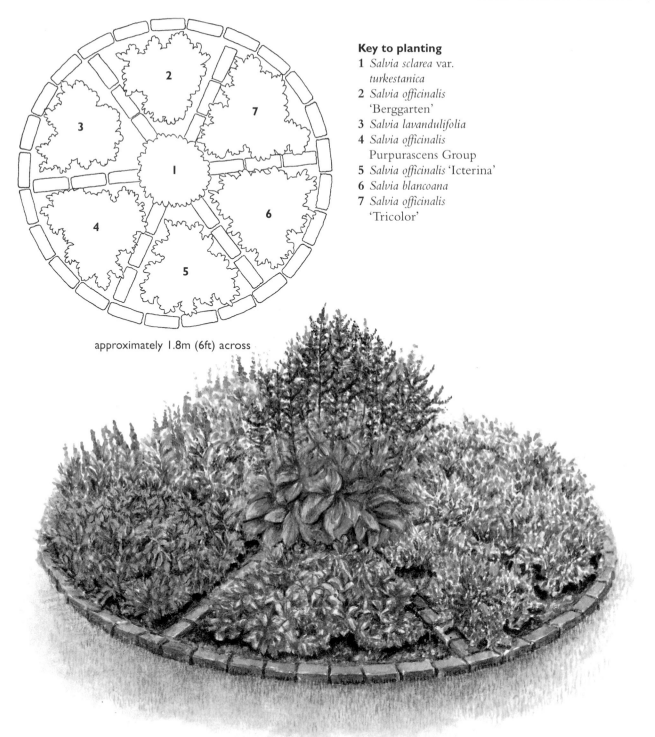

Key to planting
1 *Salvia sclarea* var. *turkestanica*
2 *Salvia officinalis* 'Berggarten'
3 *Salvia lavandulifolia*
4 *Salvia officinalis* Purpurascens Group
5 *Salvia officinalis* 'Icterina'
6 *Salvia blancoana*
7 *Salvia officinalis* 'Tricolor'

approximately 1.8m (6ft) across

drooping sheathed buds, which open into candles of pink flowers, are dramatic. A single plant, with its large rosette of toothed foliage, will make a good central plant. Alternatively, you could use the half-hardy pineapple sage (*S. elegans*), grown in an ornamental terracotta pot at the centre. This can be moved under cover in winter.

S. officinalis 'Berggarten' has large, silvery green leaves and purple-blue flowers. It contrasts well with *S. lavandulifolia*, which has thin narrow leaves with a slightly astringent, balsamic aroma. The purple foliage of *S. officinalis* Purpurascens Group provides a buffer between the greys and the golden-greens of *S. officinalis* 'Icterina'. *S. blancoana* is an unusual species with very small, narrow leaves, also balsamic in aroma. If it is to look its best, it needs the sunniest possible position, and if it is to bear its attractive but randomly appearing blue flowers, it needs a long, hot summer. Last of all is *S. officinalis* 'Tricolor', which combines silver and mauve foliage with tinges of pink, white and green. It is not quite as hardy as *S. officinalis*.

Thyme trough

Creeping thymes with their variety of foliage colour and texture, as well as the variations in flower colour, look attractive when grouped in a raised bed, trough or even on the ground in a herb wheel.

It is possible, within a relatively small rectangular trough, to display at least ten different thymes. In the centre of this arrangement, with gold, green and silver foliage respectively, are *Thymus* × *citriodorus* 'Archer's Gold', *T. serpyllum* var. *coccineus* and *T.* 'Hartington Silver'. Orange-scented *T.* × *citriodorus* 'Fragrantissimus', which will spread to about 20cm (8in), has narrow, grey-green leaves and is the main plant for one of the trough's sides. Broad-leaved thyme (*T. pulegioides*), which has lovely mauve flowers, and *T.* × *citriodorus* 'Silver Queen' are planted in the back corners, while in the front corners are *T. serpyllum* 'Minimus', which has tiny, compact leaves and small, pink flowers, and *T.* 'Doone Valley', which has gold and green variegated foliage and a lemon scent. Also included are

A collection of creeping thymes (*Thymus* spp.) makes a good show on a small scale in a trough or, if space permits, it can be allowed to spread to make a strong feature in a gravelled area.

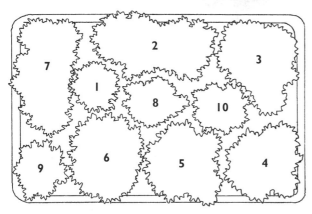

approximately 90 x 60cm (3 x 2ft)

Key to planting

1 *Thymus × citriodorus* 'Archer's Gold'
2 *Thymus × citriodorus* 'Fragrantissimus'
3 *Thymus × citriodorus* 'Silver Queen'
4 *Thymus* 'Doone Valley'
5 *Thymus herba-barona*
6 *Thymus pseudolanuginosus*
7 *Thymus pulegioides*
8 *Thymus serpyllum* var. *coccineus*
9 *Thymus serpyllum* 'Minimus'
10 *Thymus* 'Hartington Silver'

the woolly thyme (*T. pseudolanuginosus*), which will not thrive if its roots become waterlogged in wet winter weather, and *T. herba-barona*, which is noted for its aromatic caraway-scented leaves.

The success of the arrangement depends on good drainage. Keep the trough on the dry side, but remember that all plants in containers need regular watering in dry weather. Before you plant it up, position the trough in the sunniest place on a patio – remember that most thymes originate in warm Mediterranean countries. Even thymes that are native to more temperate climates, such as common thyme (*T. vulgaris*), need such a situation if they are to thrive.

Four corners of the world

Ease of access and an abundance of the herbs that are in regular use in the kitchen are among the factors that govern the design of the culinary herb garden. If you can satisfy these needs and still have an ornamental kitchen herb garden, you will have double the pleasure.

The design

To have a culinary herb garden with even greater impact, group the herbs you use frequently into the different cuisines or regions they represent or in which they originate. This garden is divided into four floating, island beds, loosely representing the four corners of the world. You could also use a design based on a square or rectangle, with paths dividing the squares.

Each bed in this design is roughly 3 × 2m (10 × 6ft 6in) and holds up to ten different herbs. The first bed, representing the East, contains herbs that will provide an oriental flavour in the kitchen and ornament in the garden. The second bed, which

Basil (*Ocimum* spp.), whether green or purple, is an essential element of Italian cooking.

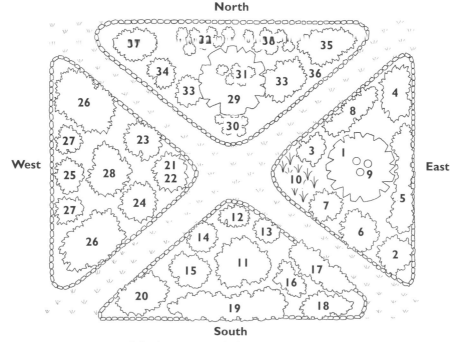

each bed approximately 3 x 2m (10ft x 6ft 6in)

Key to planting

East

1 *Morus nigra*
2 *Perilla frutescens*
3 *Ocimum basilicum* var. *citriodorum*
4 *Rheum × hybridum* (syn. *R. × cultorum*)
5 *Chrysanthemum coronarium*
6 *Brassica rapa* var. *nipposinica* (mizuna)
7 *Brassica juncea* 'Red Giant' (mustard)
8 *Brassica rapa* var. *chinensis* (pak choi)
9 *Cymbopogon citratus* (in pots)
10 *Allium tuberosum*

South

11 *Laurus nobilis*
12 *Ocimum basilicum*
13 *Origanum vulgare* 'Aureum Crispum'
14 *Origanum majorana*
15 *Satureja montana* or *S. hortensis*
16 *Allium sativum*
17 *Coriandrum sativum*
18 *Foeniculum vulgare* var. *dulce*
19 *Petroselinum crispum* var. *neapolitanum* (syn. *P. c.* 'Italian')
20 *Rosmarinus officinalis* 'Miss Jessopp's Upright'

West

21 *Capsicum annuum* var. *annuum* 'Jalapeña'
22 *Capsicum annuum* var. *annuum* 'Anaheim'
23 *Monarda citriodora*
24 *Monarda didyma*
25 *Aloysia triphylla*
26 *Tropaeolum majus* 'Whirlybird Peach Melba'
27 *Tagetes patula*
28 *Rosa virginiana*

North

29 *Sambucus nigra* 'Guincho Purple'
30 *Calendula officinalis* 'Prolifera' or Kablouna Series
31 *Primula veris* or *P. vulgaris* or both
32 *Viola tricolor* (for underplanting)
33 *Myrrhis odorata*
34 *Borago officinalis*
35 *Allium schoenoprasum*
36 *Armoracia rusticana* 'Variegata'
37 *Levisticum officinale*
38 *Sanguisorba minor*

This mixture of oriental leaves, which have been sown in blocks, can be used as a cut-and-come-again crop. Sow in succession so that you have a supply of fresh leaves over a long period.

greenhouse, and planted out when there is no further danger of frost.

There are, of course, other ways of dividing the beds. If, for example, you enjoy French, Italian, Spanish and Oriental cooking, you could arrange each bed accordingly into your favourite cuisines. There have even been designs based on single dishes, such as a pizza party bed, where each wedge of a circle, contains the herbs to suit different pizza toppings. In such specialist plantings there are bound to be overlaps, when the same herb – parsley or rosemary, for example – will occur in several of the beds, since they are so universally enjoyed.

The planting

Many of the herbs used in these four beds are half-hardy or frost-tender varieties, and they should be sown in a heated propagator in a greenhouse, potted on and planted out only when all danger of frost is over. Japanese basil (*Perilla frutescens*) and basil (*Ocimum basilicum*), in particular, need frost-free conditions. Some of the plants, such as lemon grass (*Cymbopogon citratus*) and lemon verbena (*Aloysia triphylla*), are best grown in pots and over-wintered in the greenhouse or, in the case of lemon verbena, left *in situ* and mulched with straw or agryl fleece to protect them for the cold.

Lemon grass is a tropical, rather grass-like plant, which is sold in some supermarkets for flavouring oriental dishes. You can start the plants off by putting these supermarket lemon grass 'sticks' into a glass with water to cover their ends. After a few days small white rootlets should appear. When there is a strong root system, remove them from the water and pot them up in a loam-based compost and grow them on in the greenhouse until you are ready to place them in a pot in the oriental corner.

The oriental planting shown here is made in groups, but if you have the space you could sow direct into the ground a mix of seeds, which can be harvested as a cut-and-come-again crop. You can make successional sowings in different parts of the oriental bed between other plants for an extra, yet short-term ornamental effect.

represents the South, contains a collection of herbs that bring to mind, mouth and nose the flavours and aromas of Mediterranean regional cooking. In the West are flavours and fragrances from America, including the hot spicy taste of chilli peppers. The final bed, representing the North, holds many of the herbs that could be described as signature herbs of British cuisine.

Each bed holds a tree or, in the case of the West, a rose, to provide height and a central focal point. Most of the herbs in the various collections are annuals, which are sown *in situ* or grown in the

Edible flower collection

Adding flowers to salads, cakes and desserts has gained greater acceptance in recent years, and in the herb garden there are delightfully coloured flowers aplenty that are well flavoured and, in moderation, safe to eat. The edible flower garden is probably the most ornamental part of the herb garden, since it is the one area where you will enjoy and encourage flowering. In most other parts of the herb garden you need to remove flowering stems and buds to keep the plant in leaf production, because at flowering and after, the essential oil content of the leaves is reduced.

Not only can you enjoy this part of the herb harvest in a meal, but you can also enjoy it as you walk around the herb garden, acquainting yourself with the smells and tastes of the flowers that you plan to use in different dishes. You should only eat herb flowers that you are absolutely certain are safe.

The flowers of edible herbs (those with edible leaves, that is) have similar flavours to the leaves, but their colours and shapes provide extra visual and taste sensations when you use them as garnishes in foods and drinks and in their preserved forms.

Many herb flowers provide ornament in the garden as well as adding colour and flavour to salads and summer drinks. Make sure that you use only those plants you know to be edible.

The design

A narrow rectangle, 2m (6ft 6in) wide and about 5m (16ft) long, is an ideal shape for a semi-formal but very ornamental garden, in which the appearance of the flowers can be enjoyed just as much as their flavour.

The formality comes from a short-term knot effect, made by two intersecting V-shaped lines of tightly curled moss parsley (*Petroselinum crispum*) and garlic chives (*Allium tuberosum*). The slightly raised bed is edged with rough stones or a low, brick wall. Because it is well drained and in full sun, it is a good site for the aromatic, woody herbs that enjoy the conditions of their original Mediterranean habitat.

Taller herbs, including varieties of rosemary (*Rosmarinus*) and tender sages (*Salvia* spp.), are planted at the centre of the diamond-shape made by the two intersecting V-shaped lines of parsley and garlic chives. Because the planting is asymmetrical, the small triangular areas at each side of the diamond are not even.

Annuals are sown into the two larger areas, while the smaller ones hold single plants of one species – in this design, sages – to give that side of the scheme a sense of uniformity. The largest sections of this design are framed by parsley and garlic chives on two sides and the edges of the bed on three sides. Because of their size, these areas hold the majority of edible flowering plants.

The planting

In such a design it is possible to have a single herb or small groups of particular herbs combined with their various flowering forms. For example, white-flowered sage (*Salvia officinalis* 'Albiflora') and the blue (*S. officinalis*) and mauve-pink (*S. o.* 'Rosea') forms look good together in the garden, and they will make an impact combined in salads.

Some of the plants, including French lavender (*Lavandula stoechas*), lemon verbena (*Aloysia triphylla*) and woolly thyme (*Thymus pseudolanuginosus*), need to be overwintered indoors. Tangerine sage (*Salvia dorisiana* 'Tangerine') and pineapple sage (*Salvia elegans*) should also be protected indoors in winter. As an insurance policy, take cuttings of them before you bring them in, so that you will have plenty of these attractively flowered, aromatic herbs to use next year. Cover woolly thyme and *T. doerfleri* 'Bressingham' with glass or a plastic dome to protect them in winter. Keep lemon verbena and French lavender dry in winter by mulching with straw or conifer greens. In areas that are prone to severe winters you will need to protect them in a greenhouse.

Annuals, such as pot marigold (*Calendula officinalis*) and nasturtium (*Tropaeolum majus*), will self-seed throughout the bed, and in spring you can remove those that are in the wrong place and replant the seedlings where you want them to be.

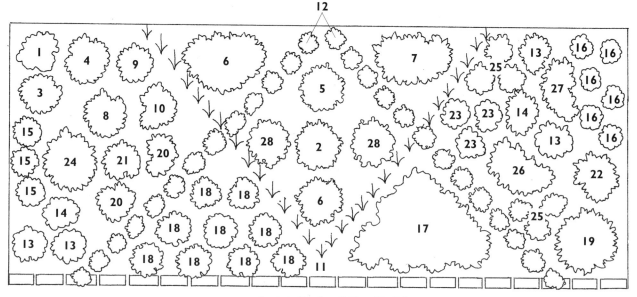

approximately 5 x 2m (16ft x 6ft 6in)

Harvest flowers for kitchen use as they come into bud and as they open. If you are going to use them fresh, pick flowers early in the day on which you intend to use them. If you are picking for preserving, pick a manageable quantity. Avoid damaged or wilted blooms and any that are infested with insects. Before use, rinse them in cool water in a basin to remove any lurking insects and lay them on absorbent kitchen paper to dry. Place them in a plastic box lined with absorbent paper and keep them in the refrigerator until you need them.

As they grow in the garden you can observe how well different coloured flowers combine with each other and with the foliage of the herbs that grow with them. One dramatic example is the cherry-red colour of the flowers of tangerine sage, standing out from the frilled, deep purple foliage of Japanese basil (*Perilla frutescens* 'Atropurpurea'). Seeing them side by side will inspire you to make interesting floral additions to your food.

Key to planting

1 *Rosmarinus officinalis* 'Miss Jessopp's Upright'
2 *Rosmarinus officinalis* 'Silver Spires'
3 *Rosmarinus officinalis* 'Majorca Pink'
4 *Rosmarinus officinalis* var. *albiflorus*
5 *Salvia elegans* 'Scarlet Pineapple'
6 *Salvia dorisiana* 'Tangerine'
7 *Salvia officinalis* 'Berggarten'
8 *Salvia officinalis* Purpurascens Group
9 *Salvia officinalis* 'Icterina'
10 *Salvia officinalis* 'Tricolor'
11 *Allium tuberosum*
12 *Petroselinum crispum*
13 *Dianthus* 'Fenbow's Nutmeg Clove'
14 *Dianthus gratianopolitanus*
15 *Viola tricolor*
16 *Viola odorata*
17 *Tropaeolum majus* 'Empress of India'
18 *Calendula officinalis* 'Fiesta Gitana'
19 *Rosa moyesii* 'Geranium'
20 *Thymus doerfleri* 'Bressingham'
21 *Thymus serpyllum* 'Snowdrift'
22 *Thymus polytrichus* subsp. *britannicus* (syn. *T. praecox* subsp. *articus*)
23 *Thymus pseudolanuginosus*
24 *Lavandula stoechas*
25 *Primula veris* and *P. vulgaris*
26 *Borago officinalis* (white- and blue-flowered forms)
27 *Aloysia triphylla*
28 *Perilla frutescens* 'Atropurpurea'

Teatime arbour

A place to take tea and a place to grow herbs for tea are harmoniously combined in a teatime arbour that is situated in a sunny site near the house at the edge of a patio.

The design

The semicircular area, which is about 7.7m (25ft) at the widest point, incorporates a seating area on a York stone pavement. A range of low-growing to medium high woody herbs, annuals, biennials and perennials fill the semicircular border, in which three sets of a post-and-rope feature appear to dip and weave through the planting. These structures provide an element of height in an otherwise fairly low-growing planting, and they support several roses (*Rosa* spp.) with teatime associations – their petals can be used to make rose petal tea and their fragrance will perfume your tea parties.

The paving of the arbour is the same as that of the patio nearer the house, and it links the two areas together.

The table and chairs need to be in keeping with the overall style of the garden. The table, which doubles as the seating area, is made from a circle of the same paving material as the patio and the floor of the arbour. The circular structure is raised on an earth-filled, brick-lined support, and its shape echoes the curved nature of the planting as a whole. At the centre of the table/seat is a space to grow a mat-forming, fragrant herb, such as camomile (*Chamaemelum nobile* 'Treneague') or a creeping thyme (*Thymus pulegioides* or *T. serpyllum*).

You could reverse the planting and use the seating area for the ground-covering herbs, making a round herb seat (see page 127) and using the central area for the table.

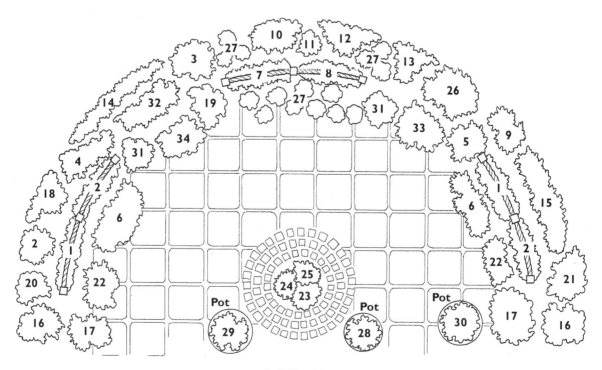

approximately 7.75 x 4.2m (25 x 14ft)

Key to planting

1 *Rosa laevigata*
2 *Rosa rubiginosa* (syn. *R. eglanteria*)
3 *Achillea millefolium*
4 *Borago officinalis*
5 *Hyssopus officinalis*
6 *Galium odoratum*
7 *Humulus lupulus* 'Aureus'
8 *Lonicera japonica* 'Halliana'
9 *Melissa officinalis* 'Aurea'

10 *Mentha spicata*
11 *Mentha crispa*
12 *Mentha × gracilis* 'Variegata'
13 *Myrrhis odorata*
14 *Petroselinum crispum*
15 *Petroselinum crispum* var. *neapolitanum* (syn. *P. c.* 'Italian')
16 *Salvia officinalis* 'Albiflora'
17 *Salvia officinalis* 'Icterina'
18 *Sanguisorba minor*

19 *Tanacetum balsamita*
20 *Monarda fistulosa*
21 *Monarda didyma*
22 *Thymus vulgaris* 'Silver Posie'
23 *Thymus × citriodorus* 'Archer's Gold'
24 *Thymus herba-barona*
25 *Thymus mastichina*
26 *Verbena officinalis*
27 *Primula vulgaris*
28 *Pelargonium* 'Graveolens'
29 *Pelargonium* Fragrans Group

30 *Aloysia triphylla*
31 *Foeniculum vulgare*
32 *Chamaemelum nobile*
33 *Rosmarinus officinalis* 'Primley Blue'
34 *Rosmarinus officinalis* 'Roseus'

The planting

The pink flowers of the briar rose (*Rosa rubiginosa;* syn. *R. eglanteria*) and the white flowers of the Cherokee rose (*R. laevigata*) are scented, as is the foliage of the briar rose, and these will provide visual delights and fragrance as you enjoy your tea. *Rosa rugosa's* large autumnal hips are supposed to be best for rose hip tea, and if you wished to grow this in addition, it could be grown as an informal hedge instead of the roses on the post-and-rope structures. If you did this, you could use the post-and-rope structures to support other climbing plants. Scented pelargoniums are grown in pots near the table/seat feature. You could also grow basil in containers and dry the foliage for later use.

Not all of the plants growing in this garden are tea plants; many are there so that you can enjoy their intrinsic beauty while you take tea. However, camomile (*Chamaemelum nobile*), fennel (*Foeniculum vulgare*), sage (*Salvia* spp.), hyssop (*Hyssopus officinalis*), lemon balm (*Melissa officinalis*), lemon verbena (*Aloysia triphylla*), mint (*Mentha* spp.), parsley (*Petroselinum* spp.), thyme (*Thymus* spp.) and bergamot (*Monarda* spp.) are among the plants from whose dried leaves, seeds or petals herbal teas can be made. Pelargonium leaves and primrose (*Primula vulgaris*) flowers can be used in baking, while borage (*Borago officinalis*) flowers are used in ice cubes to enliven summer drinks. Cucumber-flavoured borage leaves are also used in summer punches.

The golden hop (*Humulus lupulus* 'Aureus') owes its place at the tea party because it is used to make a sleep-inducing draught. Other plants to include are strawberries (*Fragaria vesca*), raspberries (*Rubus idaeus*), lemon grass (*Cymbopogon citratus*) and anise hyssop (*Agastache foeniculum*), as well as jasmine (*Jasminum officinale*).

The golden hop, *Humulus lupulus* 'Aureus', (above) will make a brightly coloured display in spring. Harvest the leaves for a soothing tea and its flowers to use in sleep pillows. Fennel, *Foeniculum vulgare*, (right) and rose petals are used to make refreshing herbal teas.

aromatic and
sensory designs

Pot pourri garden

A garden for growing the plants whose flowers or leaves will scent the house for months to come in the form of dried or moist pot pourri will bring you the satisfaction of knowing of the pleasures ahead while you enjoy the plants in the present.

The design

The garden is based on a large circle, a rectangle and a bed with curving and straight sides. From above and on the plan, it could be described as a keyhole garden, since you enter it along a path that

The dried flowers of pink hyssop (*Hyssopus officinalis* f. *roseus*), together with those of white and blue hyssop, are attractive in aromatic pot pourri.

takes you to the garden's heart. The inner, circular garden is designed to resemble a pot pourri container, holding the perfumes and aromas of the plants within it.

The edging is a mixture of plants and hard landscaping. Rope-edged tiles line the straight-sided beds, while various thymes (*Thymus* spp.) make an informal edging that spills onto the gravel path of the circular area of the garden.

A trellis encloses the beds that fringe the main path, adding a sense of intimacy and privacy to the garden. The trellis supports fragrant, white-flowered jasmine (*Jasminum officinale*) and is underplanted with lily-of-the-valley (*Convallaria majalis*). Gravel is used for the paths between the planting areas. The outer main section is edged and rather formal, but the inner circular area is not rigidly edged and creeping plants can be allowed to spill out over the gravel, making their own patterns. Stepping-stones help the gardener maintain this

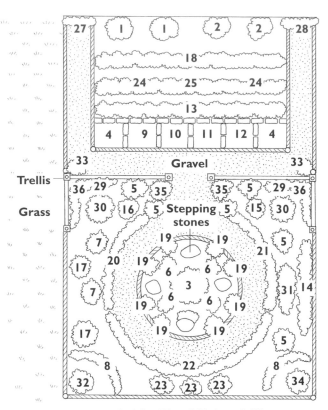

approximately 4.8 x 7.3m (15ft 9in x 24ft)

part of the garden without treading on the plants or compacting the soil.

The planting

All the plants have been chosen for their aromatic and fragrant qualities in the present, as well as for their future potential in pot pourri. In the rectangular area roses – the fragrant *Rosa gallica* 'Versicolor' and *R. rugosa* 'Alba' – are grown for their scented petals. In front of them the ground is covered by camomile (*Chamaemelum nobile*), which is sown in spring, and three species of bergamot, *Monarda fistulosa, M. punctata* and *M. didyma*. All three are attractively coloured and highly aromatic.

In small squares at the front of this bed are two blocks of *Artemisia* 'Powis Castle', whose silver foliage is perfect for drying for pot pourri. Varieties of mint (*Mentha* spp.) also grow here, but they are confined in the blocks and are allowed to spread only where you want them to go.

Height comes from the use of one or two potentially large trees, which will suit such a situation. They include juniper (*Juniperus communis*) and cider gum (*Eucalyptus gunnii*).

Crimson- and white-striped *Rosa gallica* 'Versicolor' brings both fragrance and colour to a pot pourri.

Key to planting

1 *Rosa rugosa* 'Alba'
2 *Rosa gallica* 'Versicolor'
3 *Rosa* 'Roseraie de
   l'Haÿ'
4 *Artemisia* 'Powis
   Castle'
5 *Lavandula angustifolia*
   'Imperial Gem'
6 *Hyssopus officinalis*
7 *Viola odorata*
8 *Galium odoratum*

9 *Mentha suaveolens*
10 *Mentha* × *smithiana*
   (syn. *M. rubra*)
11 *Mentha spicata*
12 *Mentha pulegium*
13 *Santolina
   chamaecyparissus*
14 *Santolina
   chamaecyparissus*
   'Lemon Queen'
15 *Nepeta cataria*
   'Citriodora'

16 *Nepeta cataria*
17 *Melissa officinalis*
   'Aurea'
18 *Chamaemelum nobile*
19 *Dianthus* 'Fenbow's
   Nutmeg Clove'
20 *Thymus herba-barona*
21 *Thymus* × *citriodorus*
   'Bertram Anderson'
22 *Thymus serpyllum* 'Vey'
23 *Salvia officinalis*
   Purpurascens Group
24 *Monarda didyma*
25 *Monarda fistulosa*

26 *Monarda punctata*
27 *Lonicera periclymenum*
28 *Lonicera japonica*
   'Halliana'
29 *Convallaria majalis*
30 *Iris germanica* var.
   florentina
31 *Ocimum basilicum*
32 *Juniperus communis*
33 *Pelargonium*
   'Graveolens'
34 *Eucalyptus gunnii*
35 *Aloysia triphylla*
36 *Jasminum officinale*

Meditation garden

Herbs, with their historic connections to medieval, cloistered, religious communities, seem natural subjects to include in a garden of meditation. Such a garden should offer calm and peace, so that you can enjoy the tranquillity without thinking about all the tasks still to be done and the harvest to be made.

The keynote of a meditation garden is a lack of variety, which can be distracting. Instead, only a few distinct species are needed to create a sense of repose, although you may need to use large numbers of plants in this restricted palette to achieve the effect you require. Nevertheless, such large-scale planting would not stimulate or excite the senses in the same way that a hot, red and yellow flower border might do.

The design

This design might fit into a garden courtyard or on a terrace that is some distance away from the main garden.

An authentic Zen garden would be enclosed by a wall or a surround of bamboo or screening to set it apart from the rest of the garden, to make sure that there is no possibility of distraction. This design is enclosed by a hedge of box (*Buxus sempervirens* 'Suffruticosa') grown to a height of 75cm (30in). This framework, complete with the shaped finials of variegated box (*B. s.* 'Elegantissima') in the corners, completely encloses a Japanese-style garden. Shaped trees, stone, raked gravel and elements of Japanese architecture are the sparse features of the garden, but, combined in this setting, they help to create a place where you can walk or stroll or sit to contemplate and clear your mind of its day-to-day clutter. In such a setting, cutting back, raking the gravel and tending the trees cease to be chores and become acts of contemplation.

The linear, rectangular shape also contributes to the sense of calm. There are no interesting curves and corners for the eye to wander into and tug the mind to follow after. Asymmetry in the arrangement of the plants and landscape elements within the garden is also important. Although

there is no doubt that this is a constructed garden, the lack of symmetry is intended to make it look as natural as possible.

Water and stone are important features in a garden of this nature, and both are achievable, even if you do not have a stream or running water. In

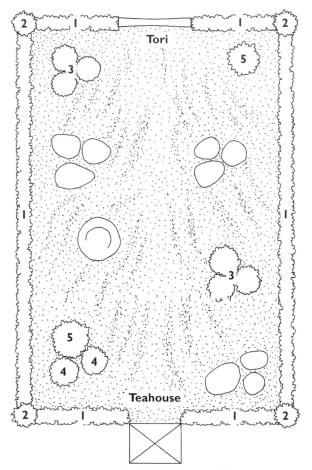

approximately 6.4 x 9.6m (21ft x 31ft 6in)

Key to planting
1 *Buxus sempervirens* 'Suffruticosa'
2 *Buxus sempervirens* 'Elegantissima'
3 *Juniperus communis* 'Hibernica'
4 *Buxus sempervirens* (topiarized as low mounds)
5 *Laurus nobilis* (shaped)

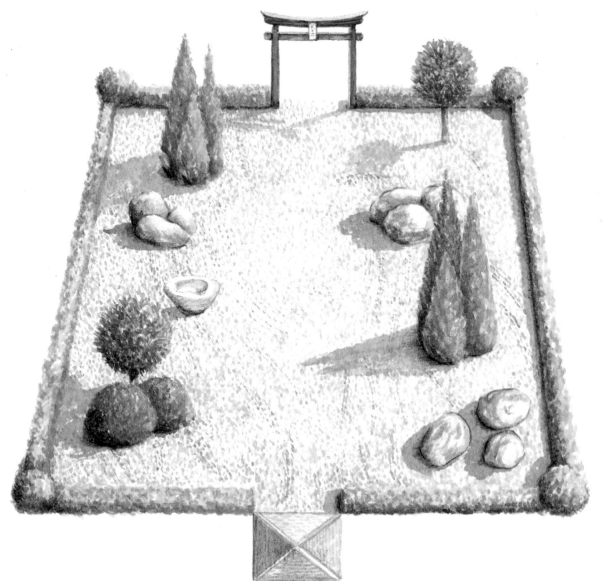

this design a hollowed-out flat stone or bowl holds a pool of water, which should be replenished when it evaporates. There is scope for pebbles, boulders and cobbles of various sizes and colours, as well as for gravel.

The central art of all Zen gardening is the ritual raking of the gravel, an activity that transforms randomly placed pieces of chippings into meticulously detailed patterns representing elements of Zen contemplation, such as flowing water. In this design the gravel is raked to look like rivers moving between the stands of shaped trees and large boulders and stones.

For best effect, raked gravel should be sited away from any deciduous trees, or the quiet contemplative activity of raking will become a chore

as you have continually to remove the fallen leaves.

The gravel layer should be built as you would a path, dug out to the total depth of material, including a layer of hardcore. At the entrance to the garden there is a wooden gateway or *tori*, typical of Japanese gardens, and at the far end of the garden is a wooden teahouse.

The planting

Evergreens such as box, juniper (*Juniperus communis* 'Hibernica') and bay (*Laurus nobilis*) are useful in this context. A suitable alternative to bay would be a graceful maidenhair tree (*Gingko biloba*). Restraint and the sparse use of plants and features are the keys to oriental meditation gardens. Shaping the plants into linear hedges, columns or round mounds is also important. This element of control is intended to keep the mind and eye from following the trails of stems and branches. Flower colour is restrained in a typical oriental garden, and here the only colour comes from the green of trees and shrubs or the colour of features such as the *tori* gateway, often red, or the teahouse at the far end of the garden. If you are fortunate and have a natural stream that can be incorporated, use a low, curved wooden bridge to make a feature instead of the teahouse.

A creeping thyme (*Thymus serpyllum* var. *coccineus*) and box (*Buxus* spp.) are the two basic plants in this tranquil setting. Pavers, with granite statuary, and gravel, which can be raked, provide the framework.

Herb pavement

A herb pavement can range from something as simple as a few plants of thyme growing in cracks in a paved path or patio or it can be an intricately laid out jigsaw of plants and pavers, making an attractive link between different areas of the house and garden.

The design

In this garden a circular area at the centre of several paths in the herb garden creates the ideal site for a number of low-growing, mound- or mat-forming herbs.

Leave a space at the centre of the circle for an architectural feature or a statuesque specimen plant, then work from there outwards, laying the natural sandstone setts into a sand and mortar base. As you lay down each inner circle of setts, leave spaces for the plants, so that the effect is of an unfinished jigsaw puzzle, with randomly placed, empty spaces.

The planting

The plants chosen for this design are all wonderfully aromatic, releasing their pungent fragrances as you brush past them, or, since some of them will take light traffic, when you walk over them. This is an opportunity to indulge yourself and to choose your favourite colours, foliage forms and shapes. In most cases you need use no more than two or three plants to gain the maximum aromatic impact.

Among the thymes used here is *Thymus* × *citriodorus* 'Silver Queen', which has a delicate silver line around the edge of each small leaf. For flower interest there is Cilician thyme (*T. cilicicus*), which has clusters of small, mauve flowers, and conehead thyme (*T. capitatus*), which bears red-edged, cone-like flower bracts.

The lavenders are *Lavandula angustifolia* 'Hidcote', a rosy-pink flower form (*L. a.* 'Rosea') and the wonderful French lavender (*L. stoechas*), which has mauve banners flying above mauve-blue flowerheads.

Soften paving, paths or patios by growing creeping, spreading plants, such as thyme (*Thymus serpyllum*) and pinks (*Dianthus* spp.) in the cracks.

In *Salvia lavandulifolia*, the Corsican or Spanish sage, lavender and sage combine to overwhelm the senses with an aroma that takes you straight out of the garden to the herb-covered hills of the Mediterranean.

In the centre of the pavement is a box (*Buxus sempervirens* 'Kingsville Dwarf'), a very slow-growing form, which may reach 1m (3ft) in time, and to bring your feet back to the herb pavement there is a clump of houseleeks (*Sempervivum tectorum*), which are the only plants in this design without fragrance, but they will creep around and over the pavement, sending out daughter plants to soften its far edges.

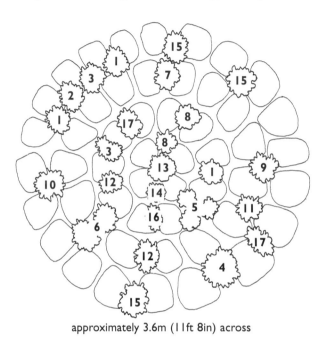

approximately 3.6m (11ft 8in) across

Key to planting
1 *Thymus × citriodorus* 'Silver Queen'
2 *Thymus capitatus*
3 *Thymus cilicicus*
4 *Thymus pulegioides*
5 *Lavandula angustifolia* 'Hidcote'
6 *Lavandula stoechas*
7 *Lavandula angustifolia* 'Rosea'
8 *Hyssopus officinalis*
9 *Hyssopus officinalis* subsp. *aristatus*
10 *Santolina chamaecyparissus* var. *nana*
11 *Santolina chamaecyparissus* 'Pretty Carol'
12 *Chamaemelum nobile* 'Flore Pleno'
13 *Buxus sempervirens* 'Kingsville Dwarf'
14 *Calamintha nepeta*
15 *Sempervivum tectorum*
16 *Salvia lavandulifolia*
17 *Mentha requienii*

Mediterranean gravel garden

A gravel garden fulfils a number of aesthetic and practical requirements in the herb garden. It creates a micro-climate that many sun-loving herbs that originate in Mediterranean regions enjoy, extending the range of plants you can enjoy in the herb garden. It may also take the place of a lawn, freeing you from the regular maintenance a lawn requires.

It also acts as a mulch, which both suppresses weeds and helps to conserve surface water to the benefit of the plants.

A gravel garden is the ideal choice for a small, sunny, town courtyard, where a lawn would be difficult to maintain. It can also be used in a larger garden, especially when you want to cut down on

A gravel path between thyme (*Thymus* spp.), rue (*Ruta* spp.) and hyssop (*Hyssopus* spp.) acts as a weed-suppressing mulch.

A raised herb garden

A raised herb garden can be a solution to the provision of a herb garden in a small town garden, and it can also be attractive to older or disabled herb enthusiasts, who want to carry on growing their own herbs for as long as possible. Raised beds can also be used to frame a patio and to delineate the boundary between garden and house. A seat and a barbecue could be incorporated into such a setting, when the raised herb bed becomes the culinary store cupboard for outdoor entertaining.

A raised bed has two main advantages: it is easier to maintain than a planting at ground level, and the plants at the front — lady's mantle (*Alchemilla mollis*), for example — can spill over to soften the edge.

Citrus-scente

Fragrance is one of the most important facto
to consider when you are putting together a co
lection of herbs. Roses (*Rosa* spp.), lilies (*Lilium*
spp.) and pinks (*Dianthus* spp.) are among the mo
fragrant of flowering plants, but there are ma
other plants that have similar fragrance notes
accents, which are often indicated in their speci
names and in their common names. The fragrar
of lemon, the essential oil that is derived fro
lemon peel (a compound called limonene), is wh
we mean when we describe a plant as 'lemo

Key to planting
1 *Laurus nobilis*
2 *Lavandula angustifolia* 'Imperial Gem'
3 *Lavandula stoechas*
4 *Thymus × citriodorus* 'Bertram Anderson'
5 *Thymus herba-barona*
6 *Foeniculum vulgare*
7 *Allium schoenoprasum*
8 *Allium tuberosum*
9 *Mentha × piperita*
10 *Allium fistulosum*
11 *Origanum laevigatum* 'Herrenhausen'
12 *Sanguisorba minor*
13 *Salvia officinalis* 'Icterina'
14 *Salvia officinalis* Purpurascens Group
15 *Mentha pulegium*
16 *Ocimum basilicum* var. *minimum*
17 *Levisticum officinale*
18 *Primula veris* and *P. vulgaris*
19 *Viola tricolor*
20 *Calendula officinalis*
21 *Ajuga reptans* 'Variegata'
22 *Artemisia alba* 'Canescens' (syn. *A. splendens*)

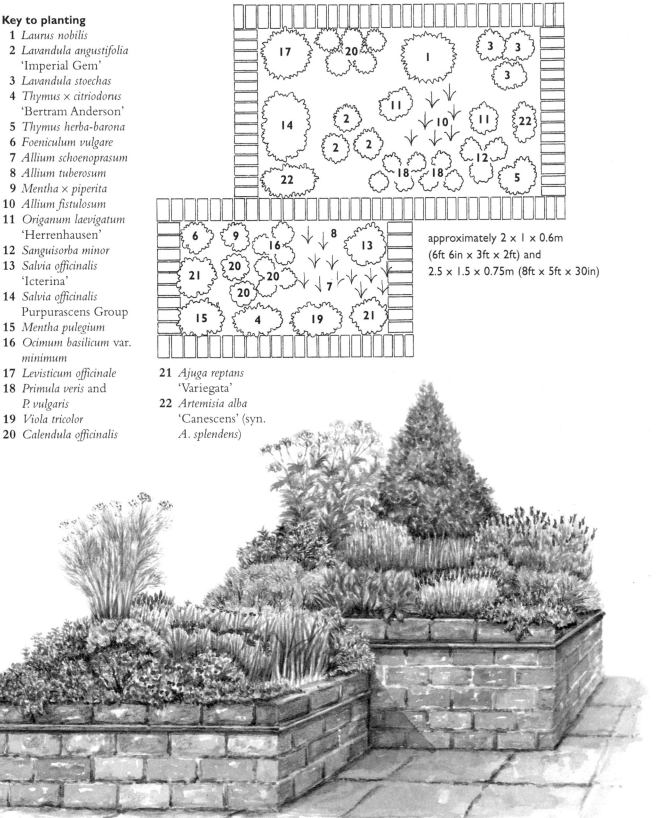

approximately 2 × 1 × 0.6m
(6ft 6in × 3ft × 2ft) and
2.5 × 1.5 × 0.75m (8ft × 5ft × 30in)

Golden variegated lemon balm (*Melissa officinalis* 'Au
is useful for its decorative, scented foliage. It forms s
stantial clumps and should be cut back after flowerin
encourage a second flush of leaves.

For ease of access, you may wish to increa[se]
height of the bed so that the soil's surface is
higher than those shown here. A brick-built
bed will be the most stable, long-lasting con[tainer]
for such a use. Old railway sleepers are popu[lar for]
making raised beds, but they are expensive a[nd not]
easy to come by.

The design

Two rectangular or oblong, brick-built bed[s, facing]
each other, making an asymmetrical featur[e. These]
could be incorporated into the patio as a[n island]
floating group of island beds or as an integr[al part]
of the patio's hard landscaping.

The beds are designed to have a la[yer of]
drainage material in the base and to allow [exces-]
sive water in times of heavy rain to drain aw[ay into]
the patio's drainage system or into the soil. [Fill the]
raised beds with a loam-based compost, en[riched]
with bulky organic matter.

A depth of 60cm (2ft) is sufficient to [allow a]
few tall herbs, such as bay (*Laurus nobil[is*) and]
lovage (*Levisticum officinale*), to introduce [height]
into the low-level profile offered by most [of the]
other plants.

A covering of gravel will not only nea[ten the]
overall appearance of the beds, but it will [act as a]
weed-suppressing mulch and as a sun-abs[orbing]
and reflecting shield.

The planting

In this design culinary herbs are combin[ed with]
ornamental plants to make an attractive an[d useful]
display. The silver-leaved artemisia (*Artem[isia]
'Canescens'*) and the variegated form o[f]

Key to planting

1 *Poncirus trifoliata*
2 *Eucalyptus citriodora*
3 × *Citrofortunella microcarpa* (syn. *Citrus mitis*)
4 *Cymbopogon citratus*
5 *Pelargonium citronellum*
6 *Pelargonium* Radula Group
7 *Pelargonium* 'Rober's Lemon Rose'
8 *Thymus* × *citriodorus*
9 *Thymus* × *citriodorus* 'Archer's Gold'
10 *Agastache rugosa* or *A. foeniculum*
11 *Mentha* × *piperita* f. *citrata*
12 *Monarda citriodora* or *M. lambada*
13 *Calendula officinalis* 'Lemon Queen'

14 *Salvia dorisiana* 'Tangerine'
15 *Melissa officinalis* 'All Gold'
16 *Aloysia triphylla*

17 *Oenothera* 'African Sun'
18 *Tagetes tenuifolia* 'Lemon Gem'

19 *Symphytum* × *uplandicum* 'Variegatum'
20 *Ocimum basilicum* var. *citriodorum*

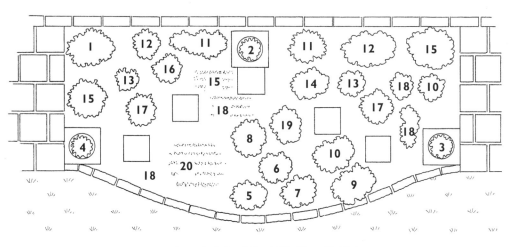

approximately 5.4 × 2.7m (17ft 6in × 8ft 8in)

Left: Grow lemons and oranges in pots so that you can move them into a frost-free site during winter. Alternatively, you can swaddle the plant and pot in a covering of horticultural fleece.

the house, the easier it will be to bring them inside in autumn.

A brick edge separates the planted border from the lawn, making mowing and general maintenance easier.

The planting

Plants such as the Japanese bitter orange (*Poncirus trifoliata*), lemon-scented gum (*Eucalyptus citriodora*), Calamondin orange (× *Citrofortunella microcarpa*; syn. *Citrus mitis*), pelargonium (*Pelargonium* spp.) and lemon grass (*Cymbopogon citratus*) are tender and should be overwintered indoors. Lemon verbena (*Aloysia triphylla*) can be protected *in situ* with a layer of straw or a mulch of horticultural fleece. Take cuttings in summer or autumn to make sure you have new plants in case it does not survive the winter, even if it has been protected, outdoors.

The lemon-scented basil (*Ocimum basilicum* var. *citriodorum*) is also tender and will have to raised in the greenhouse and planted out annually in late spring or even early summer, when all danger of frost is past. Give it the sunniest possible site, so that it becomes established quickly and forms a lime-green clump of scented foliage.

Grow *Pelargonium citronellum*, *P.* Radula Group and *P.* 'Rober's Lemon Rose', which has rosy-lemon fragrance notes, as summer bedding for an alternative to container-grown plants. Take cuttings from them in summer and autumn, and pot them up in autumn to bring indoors.

Some lemon-scented plants don't have the appropriate flower colours for this type of garden, but they should be included for their foliage. Site them carefully so that the flowers either make a dramatic statement or blend in with the rest of the planting. In this design, the sharp red flowers of *Salvia dorisiana* 'Tangerine' will provide a hot visual contrast to the near lemon-coloured annuals. The variegated foliage of Russian comfrey (*Symphytum* × *uplandicum* 'Variegatum') will also be a good foil for this bright red flower.

For visual enjoyment grow several plants with lemon or orange flowers. Pot marigold (*Calendula officinalis*), either in a mixture such as 'Fiesta Gitana', in which shades of lemon and orange are random, or 'Lemon Queen', in which lemon predominates, combined with African or French marigold (*Tagetes tenuifolia* 'Lemon Gem'), will provide a delightful splash of colour.

Providing scent and colour is a day-flowering evening primrose (*Oenothera* 'African Sun'), which has a trailing habit and which will sprawl between stepping-stones. Golden foliage, sometimes lemon-scented, as in the case of *Thymus* × *citriodorus* 'Archer's Gold', is used to continue a lemon effect. Lime green flowers will also add to the citrine effect.

Evening arbour

A herb garden has to appeal to all the senses and to have aesthetic as well as practical objectives. Perhaps none of these objectives is more important than to provide a place where it is possible to sit or walk and enjoy your handiwork, as well as the beauty of the plants. Most people's hurried lives allow for such repose only in the evenings and, fortunately, that is one of the times when colour and fragrance are at their loveliest.

As the sunlight fades, the colours of flowers alter, some decreasing in intensity and others seeming to be more emphatic. Yellow, for example, appears to hold its level, day or night, but the bright reds of the day change, darkening to shades of carmine and taking on more purple tones. Blue and white seem to become more intense, almost luminous. Fragrance behaves in a similar way, with some of the day's perfume lingering on the still, cooling air of the evening, while there are several plants whose fragrance is apparent only in the evening as they attract night-flying moths to pollinate them.

When you plan a garden to enjoy in the evening bear in mind colour and fragrance, shelter, ease of access and, above all, the need to provide a pleasant place to sit.

Plant the area near to a bench or seat that catches the last of the day's sun with fragrant plants such as roses, (*Rosa* spp.) pinks (*Dianthus* spp.) and lilies (*Lilium* spp.), so that you can enjoy their visual and aromatic pleasures.

themed
designs

Medicinal herb garden

It is known that plants were grown for medicinal purposes in the temple gardens of Ancient Egypt and that the characteristics of plants were studied in China and in Greece long before they were appreciated in Europe. It was only in the sixth century that gardens, planted specifically for the curative properties of the herbs, were attached to monasteries.

In the early physic gardens, as they were known, plants were grown for identification purposes and to assess their efficacy. Originally, the medicinal beds were laid out in straight rows, with

Angelica (*Angelica archangelica*), a biennial, is a statuesque plant, grown for its culinary and medicinal properties. Although its seedheads are attractive, they should be removed because it self-seeds abundantly.

plants grouped according to their families. If you are growing a medicinal garden for your own use, make sure that you know exactly what you are planting and that you know how to use what you grow safely. Otherwise, enjoy the plants in this medicinal garden for their ornamental attributes and their medicinal associations.

The design

Based on the checkerboard idea, this design uses the plants as the pavers, allowing them light and air to each side. Each planting area is roughly 50cm (25in) square, with enough space around it for the plant to spread. For ease of access, it is possible to move around the plants using small pavers or three bricks

The oil extracted from the seeds of borage (*Borago officinalis*) is used as an alternative to evening primrose oil in many proprietary preparations.

set into the soil. The garden is set into grass, so make sure the plants at the edges are far enough away from the lawn to make mowing the edges easy.

In this medicinal garden each plant block consists of several specimens of the same plant, so that you can see and identify them easily. If you are harvesting material from the herbs, remember to take evenly from the whole group of plants to keep the overall look of the planting even and attractive.

The planting

All of the plants used in this garden have medicinal uses, but make sure that you know exactly what you are planting and how each should be used. Yarrow (*Achillea millefolium*), for example, takes its name from the Greek Achilles, whose soldiers used it to heal their wounds; the common name, woundwort, also reflects this use. *Alchemilla xanthochlora* has been of importance in treating gynaecological problems, but it is probably more often grown for the cosmetic reason that the dew held in its mantle-like leaves was thought to be the most pure and efficacious water for washing.

Grow *Aloe vera* – whose fleshy leaves can be used in a good home remedy for burns and bites – in containers, one at each end of the garden, but remember to bring them in winter, because they are not frost hardy.

You might choose *Echinacea purpurea*, which has properties that are thought to stimulate the immune system and promote healing. It is a statuesque plant, which will make a display of coneflowers with mauve-pink or white flowers depending on variety.

Some of the plants used in this design are used in herbalism, aromatherapy and homeopathy. They include pot marigold (*Calendula officinalis*), Aaron's rod (*Verbascum thapsus*) and sage (*Salvia officinalis* 'Berggarten'). Camomile (*Chamaemelum nobile*), which is used here for its flowers, is known for the healing value of its essential oils, especially when they are used as the basis of a soothing tea. Commercially, it is used in the production of creams and ointments.

Most of the plants used are perennials or herbaceous plants, with the exception of borage (*Borago officinalis*), pot marigold and fenugreek (*Trigonella foenum-graecum*), which need to be grown from seed sown in spring.

Key to planting

1 *Achillea millefolium*
2 *Alchemilla xanthochlora*
 (syn. *A. vulgaris*)
3 *Allium sativum*
4 *Aloe vera* (in a
 container)
5 *Althaea officinalis*
6 *Angelica archangelica*
7 *Borago officinalis*
8 *Calendula officinalis*
9 *Chamaemelum nobile*
10 *Echinacea purpurea*
11 *Eupatorium perfoliatum*
12 *Filipendula ulmaria*
13 *Foeniculum vulgare*
14 *Fragaria vesca*
15 *Hyssopus officinalis*
16 *Lavandula × intermedia*
 'Grappenhall'
17 *Melissa officinalis*
18 *Mentha spicata*
19 *Primula veris* and
 P. vulgaris
20 *Rosa rugosa* 'Alba'
21 *Rosmarinus officinalis*
 'Severn Sea'
22 *Salvia officinalis*
 'Berggarten'
23 *Symphytum ×*
 uplandicum
 'Variegatum'
24 *Trigonella*
 foenum-graecum
25 *Valeriana officinalis*
26 *Verbascum thapsus*
27 *Verbena officinalis*

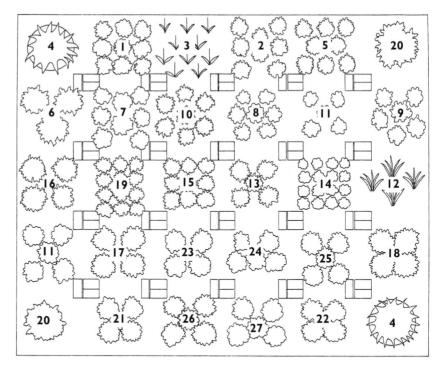

approximately 6 x 5m (19ft 6in x 16ft)

Oriental collection

This collection combines culinary, medicinal and fragrant plants that are linked by their oriental origins. Some of the plants, such as *Camellia sinensis*, are grown commercially to make tea, and they are included in this garden for their oriental connections. This design is not one to be undertaken lightly and it should be planted by a herb enthusiast who can identify and differentiate among the plants that are edible and those that are not. The

azure monkshood (*Aconitum carmichaelii*) is, for example, poisonous and must be handled with extreme care. Although this sounds alarming, once it is established and in flower, it is well worth the extra care you need to take with it.

The design

Based on a circle with a diameter of about 6m (almost 20ft), this garden has the symbolic division

The deep rust-red flowers of the day lily *Hemerocallis* 'Stafford' are edible, as are the buds and shoots. They are used, fresh or dried, in many Oriental cuisines.

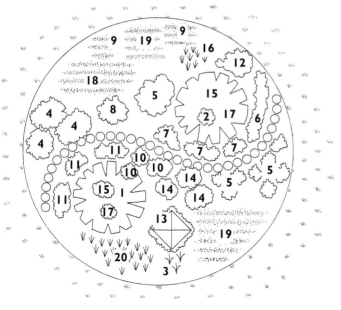

Key to planting

1 *Wisteria sinensis*
2 *Morus nigra*
3 *Allium tuberosum*
4 *Hemerocallis fulva*
5 *Paeonia lactiflora* 'Festiva Maxima'
6 *Nandina domestica*
7 *Rosa chinensis*
8 *Camellia sinensis*
9 *Papaver somniferum*
10 *Aconitum carmichaelii*
11 *Rheum × hybridum* (syn. *R. × cultorum*)
12 *Mentha* spp.
13 *Lonicera japonica* 'Halliana'
14 *Leonurus sibiricus*
15 *Gentiana burseri* var. *villarsii* (syn. *G. macrophylla*)
16 *Allium sativum*
17 *Panax ginseng*
18 *Trigonella foenum-graecum*
19 Chinese brassicas in variety
20 *Crocus sativus*

approximately 6m (19ft 6in) across

between the yin and the yang sweeping through it. This curving dividing line, which balances each part of the circle against the other, is formed by a swathe of bamboo stakes, of varying heights up to 30cm (12in). The stakes are available from garden centres and specialist suppliers, but if you cannot find them, use rounded posts cut to different lengths. The concept of yin and yang is one of balance and harmony, and the planting reflects this in the size

and shape of the plants selected for the two parts. Apart from this, however, there are no actual yin and yang elements in the plant combinations.

Use standard bamboo canes to make the wigwam support for the honeysuckle (*Lonicera japonica* 'Halliana'), which is chosen for its oriental origins and the medicinal uses of its flowers and stems.

The planting

The two major plants in this scheme are deciduous – a *Wisteria sinensis*, grown for its fragrance and shaped into a weeping standard, and a mulberry (*Morus nigra*). It will be some years before you can harvest the fruits for a dessert, but while it is growing the grey bark, statuesque shape in winter and fresh spring leaves will offer visual pleasure.

The wisteria and mulberry are underplanted with gentian (*Gentiana burseri* var. *villarsii*; syn. *G. macrophylla*), a large-leaved, upright plant, which bears blue flowers in summer, and ginseng (*Panax ginseng*), which is used in traditional Chinese medicine. Both the gentian and the ginseng occur naturally in the Chinese countryside.

Making a bold display on each side of the bamboo divide are Chinese motherwort (*Leonurus sibiricus*) and *Rosa chinensis*. Chinese motherwort is a biennial, which grows to 60–90cm (2–3ft) and has deeply cut, prominently veined leaves and delicate pink-lipped flowers arranged in whorls around the stems. It, too, has traditional uses in Chinese medicine. Nestling near to part of the bamboo divider is the sacred bamboo (*Nandina domestica*), which provides strong autumn foliage colour.

Within this planting there are many edible plants, including the fruits of the mulberry, the leaves of the garlic chives (*Allium tuberosum*), the roots, buds and flowers of day lily (*Hemerocallis fulva*) and the petals and hips of *Rosa chinensis*. The leaf tips of *Camellia sinensis* are fermented to make classic Chinese green tea, and the seeds of the opium poppy (*Papaver somniferum*) are used in baking. The stalks of the cultivated rhubarb (*Rheum × hybridum*) can be eaten, as can the flowers and leaves of the mints (*Mentha* spp.) and the bulbs of garlic (*Allium sativum*). *Panax ginseng* is used medicinally. The seeds of fenugreek (*Trigonella foenum-graecum*) are used as a spice, while the styles of *Crocus sativum* are the source of saffron. Finally, the design includes some edible Chinese brassicas.

Chinese motherwort (*Leonurus sibiricus*) has traditional uses in Chinese medicine.

Cosmetic herb garden

Set against a trellis and sheltered by a rustic brick wall, this border has an intrinsic beauty that derives from the soft informality of the old-fashioned herbs it holds. In addition, each of the plants has a traditional use in the preparation of homemade cosmetics or beauty treatments.

Most of the herbs grown in this garden are best used in herbal or floral waters or in bath bags to perfume water. Some – rosemary (*Rosmarinus* spp.) and camomile (*Chamaemelum nobile*), for example – can be used in herbal shampoos. Camomile is known for its soothing properties in bath and skin lotions as well as for the way it lightens hair. Pot marigold (*Calendula officinalis*), which is used with camomile to make a soothing skin ointment, is also included in the scheme. Lavender (*Lavandula* spp.), a plant whose name comes from the Latin word for washing or cleansing, is renowned for its antibacterial properties. Dried flowers can be used to make cleansing bath waters or incorporated in facial steams. Rosemary and sage (*Salvia* spp.) are popular for use in herb waters, as is yarrow (*Achillea millefolium*). Lady's mantle (*Alchemilla mollis*) is prized for its ruffled leaves, which hold dewdrops in the early morning.

Leaves of mint (*Mentha* spp.), added to a bowl or basin of hot water, will provide a soothing, cleansing herbal water for tired feet, while the roots of soapwort (*Saponaria officinalis*), will, as its name suggests, make a soft, safe soap.

The design

The border could be backed by a boundary wall, a fence or, as here, by a wall and trellis, which provide shelter for the border and create a room-like impression, emphasizing the indoor uses of the herbs grown within it. Although the softly curved front edge of the border is edged with a row of bricks or pavers to make a distinct mowing edge, as it is bounded by the lawn, plants are also used to make an informal edge.

The plants are arranged in groups and they vary in height from the very tall, dramatic stands of

The daisy-like flowers of camomile (*Chamaemelum nobile*) are used to make ointments and shampoos.

plants such as lovage (*Levisticum officinale*), which is used in perfumery as well as having culinary uses, to the short, mat-forming plants such as house-leeks (*Sempervivum tectorum*), which are grown for the soothing juices that are useful in the treatment of burns. The change in the height of the plants helps to create an undulating effect and gives the border more interest.

Children's garden

Introducing children to gardening in general and to herb gardening in particular is one of the most rewarding projects for parents or grandparents, with long-term good effects for the children, even if they are not entirely willing in the short term. To keep a child's interest, the garden needs to have many colourful and eye-catching plants or plants that provide fairly quick results in terms of growing and flowering. The garden needs a good shape, and it should be a fun place that the child can enjoy to be in as well as to learn from. Above all, however, it should be a safe place, so make sure that the plants you suggest are safe for children to use, In this garden poppy (*Papaver* spp.) and Aaron's rod (*Verbascum thapsus*) are the only two that children should avoid eating, but they are safe to handle, and of course, the poppy seeds can be used in bread- or biscuit-making.

Many lovely wildflowers, including daisies (*Bellis perennis*), sweet violets (*Viola odorata*) and

Mix colourful annuals, such as sunflowers (*Helianthus annuus*), with herbs and attractive vegetables, including pumpkins, to make an exciting children's garden.

approximately 5.6 x 3m (18 x 10ft)

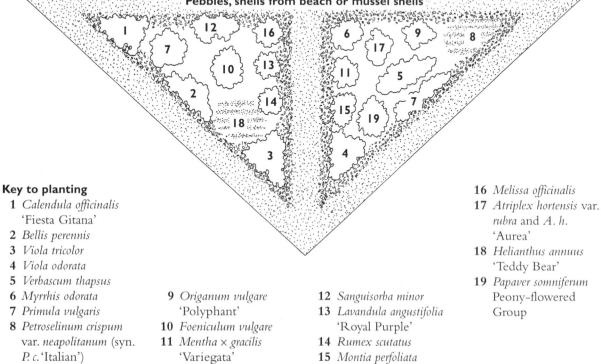

Pebbles, shells from beach or mussel shells

Key to planting

1 *Calendula officinalis*
  'Fiesta Gitana'
2 *Bellis perennis*
3 *Viola tricolor*
4 *Viola odorata*
5 *Verbascum thapsus*
6 *Myrrhis odorata*
7 *Primula vulgaris*
8 *Petroselinum crispum*
  var. *neapolitanum* (syn.
  P. c. 'Italian')

9 *Origanum vulgare*
  'Polyphant'
10 *Foeniculum vulgare*
11 *Mentha × gracilis*
  'Variegata'

12 *Sanguisorba minor*
13 *Lavandula angustifolia*
  'Royal Purple'
14 *Rumex scutatus*
15 *Montia perfoliata*

16 *Melissa officinalis*
17 *Atriplex hortensis* var.
  rubra and *A. h.*
  'Aurea'
18 *Helianthus annuus*
  'Teddy Bear'
19 *Papaver somniferum*
  Peony-flowered
  Group

Dwarf sunflowers, such as *Helianthus annuus* 'Teddy Bear', can be enjoyed by children when they are planted at the front of the garden.

heartsease (*Viola tricolor*), are among the many favourite flowers of children. These are all plants with stories and games, such as the making of daisy chains, which can be enjoyed as the garden grows.

The design

A simple geometric shape – a triangle – is divided into two smaller triangles to form the basis of the garden. Its clean lines are also reminiscent of the shape of a kite, and when the plants within it are flowering, the effect they create is of a brightly painted flag.

The beds are edged with large shells, which could be collected at the seaside. The paths, covered with cream-coloured gravel, blend well with shells of any colour. Alternatively, the edges can be made with wooden boarding and the path itself made of crushed shells. In such a large area of path it might be difficult to find sufficient shells, so you could alternate shell sections with gravel areas or with stepping-stones.

The planting

Colour in this garden comes from annuals, such as pot marigold (*Calendula officinalis* 'Fiesta Gitana'), which bring a sparkling mix of sunny oranges and bright lemon colours. The petals of pot marigold can be combined with the flowers of the daisies, violets and heartsease to add colour to salads. Other herbs supply leaves for salads, including parsley (*Petroselinum crispum*), salad burnet (*Sanguisorba minor*), red and golden orache (*Atriplex hortensis* var. *rubra* and *A. h.* 'Aurea') and buckler-leaf sorrel (*Rumex scutatus*). In winter miner's lettuce (*Montia perfoliata*) offers sharp and crunchy foliage for use in salads.

The long, black, aniseed-flavoured seeds of sweet cicely (*Myrrhis odorata*) make an excellent liquorice substitute, and their size helps children to learn about seed development. They can be seen easily and sown as soon as they are ripe and black, and by autumn they will have produced small, feathery-leaved plants.

Most of the plants within the garden are low-growing or of medium height. The levels are varied with red or golden orache (*Atriplex* spp.), which should be sown direct in the ground in late spring. Sow it in clumps the first year, and in subsequent years it will seed itself all round the garden, making random and attractive colour combinations. Aaron's rod – also known as mullein or verbascum – is a very tall, stately plant with softly textured grey leaves. In early spring caterpillars feast on the shoots, but although the leaves look worse for wear, once the caterpillars have moved into the next stage of their lifecycle, the plants always seem to regenerate and survive.

Fennel (*Foeniculum vulgare*) is another plant that offers a good height, and if it is closely planted will provide a mass of umbrella-like flowerheads all through the summer.

Some of the plants, such as lavender (*Lavandula* spp.), can be used by children to make aromatic gifts for parents and friends. Lavender flowers, dried in bunches or singly, can be used to make scented linen bags. Stems of lemon balm (*Melissa officinalis*), tied with pretty ribbons, will be relaxing herb bundles for bathtime, while kitchen herbs – parsley, mint (*Mentha* spp.) and oregano (*Origanum vulgare* 'Polyphant'), for instance – can be used to make fresh or dried bunches for use in cooking.

Wildlife garden

Gardens are often incidental havens for wildlife, filled with bee- and butterfly-attracting flowering plants, as well as providing shelter, water and food all through the year, particularly in winter.

Gardens are becoming increasingly important for both plants and animals, and the herb garden, with its predominance of wildflowers and native plants, is particularly well-suited to supporting a wide range of wildlife, while offering an informal, relaxed style.

Wildlife in the form of bees, butterflies, birds, insects and amphibians adds a lively dimension to the garden, providing movement and song, as well as colour.

A wildlife garden isn't necessarily untidy and it need not take up the whole garden, but it will certainly reward your efforts when it is established.

Watermint (*Mentha aquatica*) and fool's watercress (*Apium nodiflorum*) grow well in the water and at the waterside, and will spread and self-seed around the water's edge. If clumps become too dense and overpower other plants, divide them.

The design

This wildlife garden is sited at the boundary of the garden where it can be a distinct, almost secret haven for humans and wildlife. The central feature is a small pond, which can be reached by means of a stepping-stone pathway. Pebbles and larger stones drift from the border to the water's edge, creating an informal effect. The pond should be in a sunny situation, and it does not have to be large to attract a good range of insects, amphibians and birds. Avoid steeply sloping sides, and instead aim to provide a gently sloping, shallow-edged pond that you can plant up with marginal plants, which don't mind having moist roots. At its deepest it should be at least 46cm (18in) deep so that it doesn't freeze up in winter.

The planting

Trees and shrubs predominate at the far side of the design, where a grove of three birches (*Betula pendula* 'Laciniata') and a lime tree (*Tilia cordata*) provide stems, foliage, seeds and flowers to attract a range of insects and birds through the year. At their base, plantings of cowslip (*Primula veris*) and woodruff (*Galium odoratum*) provide ground cover and attractive spring flowers.

The purple elder (*Sambucus nigra* 'Guincho Purple') also provides height as well as nectar for insects and berries for birds. Foxgloves (*Digitalis purpurascens*), bergamot (*Monarda didyma*) and anise hyssop (*Agastache foeniculum*) are bee- and butterfly-attracting plants, while fennel (*Foeniculum vulgare*) seems to act as a magnet for hoverflies, which do much good in the garden as natural predators of pests such as aphids. Hyssop (*Hyssopus officinalis*) and thyme (*Thymus* spp.) are similarly powerful bee-attracting plants, and hyssop also attracts lacewings. Here the hyssop is planted as an informal border plant, while the different thymes makes mats of ground cover between the stepping-stones. Honeysuckle (*Lonicera periclymenum*), which winds through the lime tree, lavender (*Lavandula* spp.), pot marigold (*Calendula officinalis*) and nasturtium (*Tropaeolum majus*) are all good nectar plants, but many also attract hoverflies and are food plants for different stages of butterfly lifecycles.

Bees and butterflies will enjoy the flowers, and birds, especially finches, will be attracted to the seedheads of teasel (*Dipsacus fullonum*). The seeds of

The small, yellow-green flowers of dill (*Anethum graveolens*) are a magnet for hoverflies all through the summer.

chicory (*Cichorium intybus*) are also useful for a number of birds in autumn.

To keep the garden full of colour and attractive visually to you as well as to the wildlife, prepare the site well in late summer when you put the pond in place. In autumn plant up the shrubs, trees and perennial herbs. In spring sow the hardy annuals directly into the ground. Once the plants are growing well and the site is well-watered, mulch it with gravel or with bark chippings to help suppress weeds and conserve moisture.

In most herb gardens foliage and flowers are cut for use in the kitchen or to make herbal preparations. In this garden, however, you should leave the plants to flower and to produce seeds or fruit so that all parts will have some use for the wildlife that is attracted to it. Cut back the plants only when they begin to look leggy and unkempt. In spring cut back any remaining seedheads and remove self-sown plants that are surplus to your needs.

Key to planting

1 *Iris pseudacorus*
2 *Mentha aquatica*
3 *Mentha pulegium*
4 *Agastache foeniculum*
5 *Hesperis matronalis*
6 *Lavandula × intermedia* 'Grappenhall'
7 *Hyssopus officinalis*
8 *Foeniculum vulgare*
9 *Monarda didyma*
10 *Thymus vulgaris*
11 *Thymus serpyllum*
12 *Thymus herba-barona*
13 *Sambucus nigra* 'Guincho Purple'
14 *Satureja thymbra*
15 *Salvia officinalis*
16 *Salvia sclarea* var. *turkestanica*
17 *Tropaeolum majus* 'Whirlybird Peach Melba'
18 *Verbascum thapsus* or *V. chaixii*
19 *Oenothera biennis*

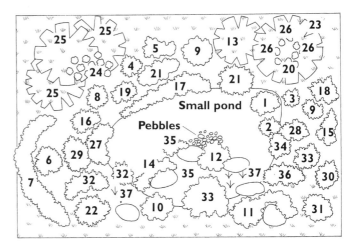

approximately 6 x 9m (19ft 6in x 29ft 6in)

20 *Lonicera periclymenum*
21 *Digitalis purpurea* f.*albiflora*
22 *Nepeta × faassenii*
23 *Tilia cordata*
24 *Primula veris*
25 *Betula pendula* 'Laciniata'
26 *Galium odoratum*
27 *Filipendula ulmaria*
28 *Eupatorium purpureum*
29 *Cichorium intybus*
30 *Dipsacus fullonum*
31 *Taraxacum officinale*
32 *Tanacetum parthenium*
33 *Origanum vulgare*
34 *Pulmonaria officinalis*
35 *Fragaria vesca*
36 *Calendula officinalis*
37 *Crocus sativus*; *C. vernus*

Foliage garden

The leaves of most herb plants are important for the flavours and colours they add to food, and often the beauty of their form, texture and colour is regarded as of secondary importance. Once you begin to look closely at the foliage of your favourite herbs, however, you cannot fail to be struck by the variety of the shape, colour, size and texture, as well as the overall effect they make.

Some herbs – rosemary (*Rosmarinus* spp.), thyme (*Thymus* spp.), sage (*Salvia* spp.) and bay (*Laurus nobilis*), for example – are evergreen and their foliage effects can be enjoyed all through the year as they provide a framework for the herbaceous perennial and annual flowering herbs. Others make a dramatic statement with their foliage. Clary sage (*Salvia sclarea* var. *turkestanica*), for instance, has silvery green, softly textured large leaves, which seem to be outlined with a dark, thin line.

The design

A trio of curved shapes, a sort of tricunx, has been chosen to hold plants selected for their foliage effects. From above, the planting plan has an almost, palmate, leaf-like structure. The largest curved area is a circle. Two roughly semicircular sections fit against it, and each section is separated from the others by rows of bricks, set lengthways, side-by-side or end-to-end.

Each circular section has a strong foliage point. The columnar juniper (*Juniperus communis*) makes an evergreen, aromatic, upright shape in one section. In the circle the mulberry (*Morus nigra*), with its grey bark and lime green foliage in late spring is attractive in any season. Balancing these two trees is the herbaceous ornamental rhubarb (*Rheum palmatum*), which has red prickles arming its stems and large green and russet palm-shaped leaves.

The planting

In this design plants with a wide range of leaf shapes, sizes, colours and textures have been chosen. Garlic chives (*Allium tuberosum*), with their flat, strap-like leaves, and ordinary chives

(*A. schoenoprasum*), with their rolled leaves, are used to make contrasting informal edging plants for the large circular section. Parsley (*Petroselinum crispum*), with its deeply curled, almost moss-like leaves, is also used as an informal edge. Creeping plants with aromatic, as well as finely cut foliage, such as lady's bedstraw (*Galium verum*), alpine lady's mantle (*Alchemilla alpina*) and strawberries (*Fragaria vesca*), produce mats of contrasting foliage shapes. Creeping camomile (*Chamaemelum nobile* 'Treneague') is also used in this way, making a double offering of fragrance and leaf shape to the design.

Mounding plants, including lemon balm (*Melissa officinalis* 'Aurea') and sweet cicely (*Myrrhis odorata*), offer a range of leaf shape from fern-like through to toothed in the section that features the upright juniper. Chinese motherwort (*Leonurus sibiricus*), which has deeply indented and toothed leaves, adds to the mounded effects.

The last section holds plants with unusual foliage colour. The purple sage (*Salvia officinalis*

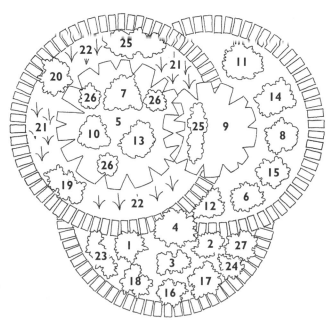

approximately 6 x 6m (19ft 6in x 19ft 6in)

Key to planting

1 *Salvia officinalis* Purpurascens Group
2 *Salvia sclarea* var. *turkestanica*
3 *Rosmarinus officinalis* 'Sissinghurst Blue'
4 *Rheum palmatum*
5 *Morus nigra*
6 *Mentha × piperita*
7 *Mentha pulegium*
8 *Leonurus sibiricus*
9 *Juniperus communis*
10 *Fragaria vesca*
11 *Melissa officinalis* 'Aurea'
12 *Myrrhis odorata*
13 *Chamaemelum nobile* 'Treneague'
14 *Artemisia dracunculus*
15 *Artemisia* 'Powis Castle'
16 *Santolina rosmarinifolia* subsp. *rosmarinifolia* (syn. *S. viridis*)
17 *Angelica archangelica*
18 *Angelica atropurpurea*
19 *Alchemilla mollis*
20 *Alchemilla alpina*
21 *Allium schoenoprasum*
22 *Allium tuberosum*
23 *Thymus vulgaris* 'Silver Posie'
24 *Thymus serpyllum* 'Russetings'
25 *Petroselinum crispum*
26 *Galium verum*
27 *Sanguisorba minor*

Although the flowers of sage (*Salvia* spp.) and oregano (*Origanum* spp.) are attractive, here it is the foliage that plays the important role. The small golden leaves of oregano combine well with the large, purple foliage of sage and make their own display as they weave through the sage.

Purpurascens Group), bright green cotton lavender (*Santolina rosmarinifolia* subsp. *rosmarinifolia*) and purple angelica (*Angelica atropurpurea*) stand out from the silver of clary sage and the lemon-green angelica (*A. archangelica*), while silver-edged *Thymus vulgaris* 'Silver Posie' and the dainty *T. ser-* *pyllum* 'Russettings' contrast well with each other. Although many of these herbs produce attractive flowers through the summer, their foliage can be relied on for a year-round effect, except in winter, when the evergreens hold the centre ground with their smooth, leathery leaves.

One-colour designs

Colour from flowers and foliage is probably the most important design factor when any grouping of plants is being considered. Colour combinations are subjective, however, and they work in different ways in different conditions, such as shade or full sun. Most gardeners prefer to use a wide range of colours in their gardens, but if you have the space and can afford to be selective in your choice, you could opt for a monochromatic scheme. Such a border is based on the assumption that one colour predominates. It needs to be carefully planned so that there is a succession of the chosen colour through the season.

Shades of purple are the one-colour offerings of French lavender (*Lavandula stoechas*), alliums and irises. Although the flowers are predominantly of one colour, the effect is never dull, largely because of the variations in the background foliage colour.

special features

Marking out a circle

Use a central marker cane to fix the position of the centre of the circle, then tie to it a piece of string that is, in effect, the length of the radius of the circle. Attach a second cane to the end of the string and walk in a circle, pulling the string taut and using it as a guide, and putting the second cane into the soil at regular intervals. These holes mark the outer edge of the circle.

If you want to grow plants in wedge-shaped segments, you need to divide the circle into four and then to sub-divide those four segments into half again, so that you end up with eight equal sections. You can mark the line of each of the sections with a trickle of sand. Once you have marked the basic shapes, you can put in dividing lines with brick or stepping-stones, or you can plant a line of hedging, such as box. The next step is to plant up each section according to your design.

Planting a circular bed

It is tempting to plant a circle with tall, statuesque accent plants at the centre and low-growing plants at the front edge. More pleasing, however, is an arrangement that encourages the eye to wander

Marking out a herb wheel

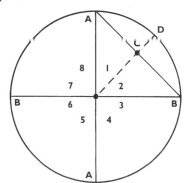

Insert a cane at the centre of the area and attach string, the same length as the proposed radius of the circle, to the cane. A second cane, tied to the other end of the string, can be used to mark the edge of the circle and divide the circle into equal segments. Alternatively, fill a bottle with sand and attach the bottle with string to a fixed point within the garden. Varying the position of the fixed point and the length of the string that is attached to the second cane or the bottle will enable you to 'draw' smooth curves on the ground. Always plan your design on graph paper before you begin.

Herb wheel variation

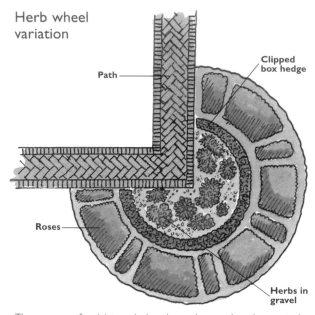

The corner of a right-angled path can be used as the central point of a herb wheel, even though only a portion of the wheel can actually be used for herbs.

over a variety of heights at the front and centre of the circle, so that it is necessary constantly to adjust to the changes in height and position of a variety of plants. It also means that you have to walk around and close to the circular design to appreciate it to the full.

Creeping thyme (*Thymus serpyllum*) in different colour form is particularly attractive if it is used to create asymmetrical, swirling patterns within a circle. A circular shape is also useful for a fragrant herb lawn of camomile or creeping thyme (see page 117). The herb lawn can be enclosed by a rim of bricks or other paving material and used partially for walking on as well as for sitting or lying on.

Given the rampant habit of mint, a herb wheel is an ideal growing space for a collection of mints (*Mentha* spp.). Instead of using brick or box as an edging, sink some slates into the ground so that the mints are partially contained. Use peppermint, eau-de-cologne mint, variegated apple mint, spearmint, gingermint, Moroccan mint, curly mint and apple mint as your mint selection and enjoy their varied foliage, flowers and aromas.

A cartwheel, perched on a circle of bricks, is the perfect outline for a small, circular herb garden.

Marjoram, golden marjoram, rue, hyssop and fennel have spread to make a wedge-shaped planting in a circular, paved area.

circular. At each stage, use the spirit level, resting on the straight-edge, which should be lying across sets of pegs. When each reading is level, you can begin digging out the ground.

Tread the ground in by walking over it or, if it is possible to move a roller on site, compact the soil with this. If you are laying the pavement straight onto the soil, remove any lumps and bumps and fill them with compacted soil.

Put in place a layer of hardcore and tamp it down. Cover the hardcore with a layer of sand. Then mix up mortar, using 1 part cement to 6 parts sand and shingle mixed. Place a dab or two of mortar in position where the paving or hard landscaping material is to go. If you are using patio pavers, five dabs of mortar are needed. Lay the paving in place and check that it is level, using the spirit level again. Continue to lay the rest of the pavement, but leave areas where you have decided to set in plants free of the mortar.

The pavement will look like an unfinished jigsaw puzzle until you add compost and grit to the hardcore and sand level. This will make an excellently drained growing medium for many of the Mediterranean herbs, such as thyme and lavender, that will grow well in a pavement such as this.

When the mortar under the paving has set, which will take about 36 hours, depending on the weather conditions, brush a dry mortar mix between the pavers. Water it in using a watering can with a fine rose.

After a few days, when the pavement is firmly bedded in you can begin to plant up the spaces with low-growing herbs.

Designs of pavements

You may wish to make a design in a separate material to the basic pavement and allow vigorous self-seeding plants, such as lady's mantle (*Alchemilla mollis*) and fleabane (*Erigeron*), to make their own patterns across the pavement.

Diamonds, suns, moons, stars and crescents, such as those shown in the plans for the evening arbour (see page 79), can be set into a dry mortar mix. Use pebbles of a different colour to make the background. Crushed shells, slates, gravel in different colours and local natural stones, particularly if they are well-weathered and easy to walk on, are all useful for the creative pavement artist.

Gravel gardens

Gravel has become a popular mulch for drought-resistant planting schemes, as well as a decorative design feature in such plantings. In a herb garden, where many of the plants will have originated in countries with warm climates, gravel is a natural choice to create the appropriate visual and environmental surroundings.

When it is laid as a mulch on top of the soil among the plants, gravel reduces water evaporation from the surface of the soil. It also acts as a weed

Many plants, such as lady's mantle (*Alchemilla mollis*), thyme (*Thymus* spp.) and purple-leaved plantain (*Plantago major* 'Rubrifolia'), will seed themselves into the gravel to make their own design. Leave a few and remove unwanted seedlings.

Chives (*Allium schoenoprasum*), although perennial, die back in winter and their edging role is lost. Nonetheless, their upright, rolled, tubular leaves and mauve pompon flowers make such an attractive display that they are worthwhile, even if only in spring and summer. Lady's mantle (*Alchemilla mollis*) is also often used for edging, but it, too, dies down significantly in winter.

Hard edges

There are several materials that can be used to make informal edges for a border or a herb garden planting. In a cottage garden or informal setting large round stones make an effective edge, and they will allow foliage and runners of plants at the front of the bed to flow through them attractively.

Low willow hurdles can be inset into the soil at the front of the bed, and they will hold up plants that flop over the edge of the lawn without detracting from the cottage or rustic look of the garden.

You can also raise the level of the bed by setting rounded timber posts or thick bamboo posts into the soil. They will keep the plants off the lawn or the edges of a path, and hold them at a higher level, where you can enjoy their flowers and foliage even more.

Hedging

Hedging in a herb garden plays much the same role as in any garden. One of its main functions is to provide shelter from the wind for the plants that grow within it. Indirectly, this shelter makes the area warmer, because it helps to prevent heat loss from the soil and to maintain the temperature of the air around the plants. Hedging not only acts as a framework and background foil for the plants that grow against it, but it also provides a unifying theme that helps to draw the elements of the herb garden together into a single whole, rather than allowing them to be viewed as individual elements in a wider landscape.

In herb gardens several plants are traditionally used for hedging. Box (*Buxus* spp.) and yew (*Taxus* spp.), two evergreen, slow-growing but hardy shrubs or trees, have long associations with cloistered herb gardens. Their foliage, closely packed on shrubby stems, makes a dense evergreen canvas against which the herb gardener can create a striking picture.

The very erect form of rosemary, *Rosmarinus officinalis* 'Miss Jessopp's Upright', with its blue summer flowers is also useful. Upright rosemary, box and yew will all tolerate hard pruning to keep them in good shape, and they can be clipped to form topiary features.

Lavender (*Lavandula* spp.) can also be used as an edging plant or to make an attractive hedge. The uniformity of colour and height make it ideal for both formal and informal beds, and there are heights and flower colours to suit a variety of situations. There is the added bonus of the fragrant summer flowers. The plants need regular light trimming once the flowers are over and again in spring.

Hedges for formal parterres and knot gardens are usually made using a palette of grey, green and golden herbs, which can all be closely clipped to provide ribbons of colour. Cotton lavender (*Santolina* spp.), which is available in a feathery-fine, silver form as well as a smooth, shiny green form, is particularly effective as a 'plant ribbon'.

Planting a hedge or an edging

Even though the finished heights of the hedge and the edge will probably be quite different, the basic planting principles are the same. Set the hedging or edging plants into holes dug along a straight line, the length of the area you want to enclose. The plants need to be spaced evenly along the line, usually two-thirds their eventual height apart, so that they can grow together to fill the space.

Measure out how many planting holes you need, unless you are planting a long boundary hedge, in which case it is easier to dig the plants in along the line, using a rough indicator, like a piece of wood, to gauge the spacing. Place a handful of fertilizer into each planting hole or fork in bulky organic matter. Make sure the hole is large enough to hold the plant's root system. Water individual plants in well.

The best time to plant a herb hedge is in autumn or spring, but whenever you plant, you will need to have available a shelter for the new hedge, because cold drying winds and harsh frosts can damage young plants.

Box (*Buxus* spp.) is one of the most popular edging plants for gardens because it responds so well to regular clipping and shaping.

Making a herb seat

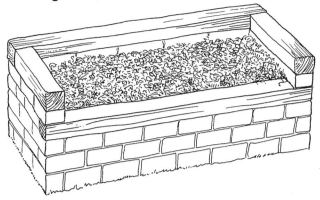

A free-standing seat can be created with brick retaining walls and a timber surround so that the surface can be planted with low-growing herbs.

Alternatively, build the seat so that the 'back' is formed by an existing brick or stone wall.

Making a herb seat

If you have a bank or an existing wall, the simplest way to make a herb seat is to use the bank or wall as the back support of the seat. On a bank-side site you will need to cut out and remove enough soil to make space for one or two people to sit comfortably.

The bare soil at the base and the soil at the back will be planted up with fragrant herbs, but before you begin preparing the soil or planting, you will need to shore up the back area. Take a piece of green horticultural netting and cut several rows of evenly spaced holes, through which you will be able to plant the fragrant herbs. Spread the netting across the back of the bank, keeping it as taut as possible. Then fix it in place with tent pegs or skewers. Use a trowel or dibber to make planting holes where the rows of holes appear on the netting.

Water the plants well, then plant them into the soil behind the netting holes. Once the back planting is done, you can begin on the base of the seat. Here you can lightly fork over the soil, add bulky organic material and then rake over the surface, before making planting holes and putting the herbs into place. Water them in well and, if necessary, give the herbs in the back of the seat a fine spray of water. Take care that you do not overwater this area in case there is a small land- and plant-slide.

The idea of a camomile seat has been taken further and converted into a fragrant bed on which to relax.

If you are using a wall as the back rest, build up a three-sided, raised bed in front of the wall. You can use old railway sleepers, large, even-sided rockery-type rocks or a simple brick wall. Whatever materials you choose, make sure the structure is safe and secure before you fill the rectangle it forms with the wall, using rubble for drainage and compost for the plants.

Once the structure is in place and the planting area filled with compost, water it well and allow it to settle before planting. It may be necessary to add more compost. If so, leave it to settle again. When the compost has settled, firm it gently and begin the planting. Make evenly spaced holes in rows and then put the plants in position.

All the plants will need regular watering until they have established themselves. Postpone the pleasure of sitting on the herb seat for a few months until the plants are growing well and the soil's surface has been completely covered with a carpet of fragrant herbs. Then you can relax, sit and enjoy the visual and the aromatic delights of the herb garden.

Plants to use include creeping thyme (*Thymus serpyllum*), camomile (*Chamaemelum nobile* 'Treneague') and creeping mint (*Mentha requienii*). Place lilies in pots on the ground so that when you are sitting, they are at nose height, and, if you wish, add a light wooden pergola to frame the seat. Grow jasmine against the trellis so that it perfumes the air around your head.

Herb lawns

Some low-growing, creeping herbs, such as the many varieties of *Thymus serpyllum* and the non-flowering form of camomile (*Chamaemelum nobilis* 'Treneague'), are hard wearing enough to be used to make small-scale lawns or paths that are not subject to heavy traffic.

The herb lawn is a useful device for altering the texture of a small area in the herb garden. The feathery leaves of camomile or the broader leaves of the creeping thyme, and later the mauve, white or pink flowers of the thyme, offer a different visual pleasure than if grass, gravel or paving have been used. The extra delight that many low-growing herbs offer, of course, is the powerful aromatic oils in their leaves, which when trodden on, are crushed and the heady fragrance released into the air.

In a small garden, a herb lawn is a viable project, but in a larger space, the maintenance of a herb lawn is labour intensive and time consuming. Any weeds that encroach have to be removed by hand and in autumn leaves from deciduous trees will have to be removed by whatever method is feasible. Raking is not easy because it may damage the herbs.

If you have a large area and are determined to have a fragrant lawn, consider planting the herb lawn in metre- (yard-) square blocks, rather like a checkerboard pattern, with the spaces between taken by grass. Another possibility is to use grass and camomile together to make a mixed lawn, with a fragrant overtone, but when you mow, remember to keep the height of cut in the region of 4–5cm (1½–2in), or you will remove the foliage that offers the fragrance underfoot.

A successful camomile lawn needs cool, shady conditions and a moist soil, while a thyme planting will do best in hot, sunny conditions in a relatively dry soil.

Preparing a site for a herb lawn

If you are starting from scratch with an area that has previously been an ordinary turf lawn, it is best to plan ahead and do the preparation well in advance, probably in the autumn or winter before you begin planting.

Remove the turf, dig out a trench and double dig the site, adding well-rotted compost to each trench. Remove large stones and any perennial weeds roots that may have been in the turf mixture. If you are simply turning an already cultivated piece of land into a herb lawn, the preparation is much the same, but it is possible to use a systemic weed killer to shorten the preparation time.

Add horticultural grit to the soil and then allow it to settle over the winter. In spring, when you are ready to begin planting, remove any annual weeds that may have begun to germinate and rake the surface level.

You will need roughly 40 plants per square metre (square yard) to make a good covering. Place the plants on the soil surface so that they are 15–30cm (6–12in) apart. It is best to plant them in rows that are staggered, so that there is space around each plant for it to spread.

Make individual planting holes for each plant, sprinkle a little fertilizer into the base of each hole, set the plants in position and water them in well. They will need regular watering until they are established, which will take two or three months.

Avoid walking on the herb lawn until the plants have formed a good mat of ground cover.

Maintaining the herb lawn

Thyme and mint will form low mats that will not require cutting A camomile lawn can, if it is a fairly small area, be cut with shears. However, a larger area will have to be mown, with the cutting blades set at a height of 5cm (2in). Remove lawn weeds by hand. If perennial weeds such as buttercup or couch grass do take hold and overwhelm the camomile or thyme, the solution is to start again. Dig out the weeds and herbs. Try to salvage some of the herbs, then replant once all the weeds are removed.

A thyme bank is a useful solution for a slope that is difficult to mow. It will also tolerate light traffic and is a fragrant place on which to rest for a while – if you can avoid the bees that it attracts.

Suitable plants

In addition to the traditional camomile, there are a number of plants that are useful and fragrant for a herb lawn. Several mints, including Spanish mint (*Mentha requienii*) and creeping pennyroyal (*M. pulegium*), will make a good ground cover and when walked on will release their aromatic oils. Mints do best in semi–shade and a relatively moist soil.

Creeping thyme (*Thymus serpyllum*), with its small mauve-pink flowers is one of the prettiest plants, as well as one of the most aromatic, for a herb lawn. Because of the different coloured flowers found within this species, it is possible to plant attractive circles within circles of thyme, which, when in flower, will look like flavoured swirls of ice cream.

Trees in the herb garden

Herbs are usually thought of as low-growing, soft-stemmed flowering herbaceous perennials, annuals and biennials. There are, however, many trees and shrubs which have traditional and modern roles to play in the pharmaceutical sector, in the home and in the herb garden.

It may not be possible to grow more than one tree in your garden, because of the tree's eventual size. However, there are several that are traditional herb garden plants, and many of these are used in severely restricted forms in containers, cut into topiary shapes or clipped and sheared annually to make attractive features in parterres and knot gardens, and used for edging and hedging. Bay (*Laurus nobilis*), yew (*Taxus baccata*) and box (*Buxus* spp.) are familiar to the herb gardener in a range of guises, from shaped container plants through to hedging and edging plants. Elders (*Sambucus* spp.), in its common form, as well as purple or golden variants, make attractive and useful trees in the ornamental herb garden.

Many other trees, including several that thrive in temperate climates, offer shade, height and ornament, as well having medicinal associations. The linden or lime (*Tilia cordata*), in particular, is one to grow for its summer flowers, which are used to make a relaxing tea.

Fruit-bearing trees, such as the mulberry (*Morus nigra*), crab apple (*Prunus malus*) and quince (*Cydonia oblonga*), as well as many nut trees, including hazel (*Corylus avellana*) and walnut (*Juglans regia*), may be the ideal choice for your garden, giving you herbal connections, use and ornament.

Creating shelter

If your garden is in a windswept area you may be able to provide shelter at the far boundary by planting several trees to provide a wooded belt. Try to choose trees for their compatibility with each other, as well as with the site. Berry-bearing trees, such as the rowan (*Sorbus aucuparia*) and hawthorn (*Crataegus monogyna*), will offer bare stems in winter, good spring foliage, attractive flowers and late-summer berries or fruits, as well as autumn foliage colour. Fruiting trees, including the sloe or blackthorn (*Prunus spinosa*) and bullace (*Prunus institia*), will also be effective.

Willow (*Salix alba*) is another appropriate choice, and it can be woven into a living hedge, as well as persuaded to create a secret garden arbour or gazebo for children. A nut walk, lined with hazel trees (*Corylus avellana*) will also provide shelter, as well as useful long hazel poles to convert into tripods or wigwams as supports for climbing plants. For a bright show in spring, underplant the hazels with cowslips. A mixed hedgerow, however, complete with dog roses for scarlet red autumn hips, honeysuckle and wild clematis or traveller's joy, would be the perfect choice for the complete herbal shelter.

Planting trees

While you are preparing the planting hole for a specimen tree or several holes for a boundary hedge, remember to keep the plants sheltered from drying wind, with their roots in water or wrapped in moist hessian.

Dig a hole large enough to take the tree's roots comfortably. Scatter a handful of slow-release fertilizer into the base of the planting hole. Place the tree into the hole, backfill with soil, then firm down the soil around the tree. Water the plant in well, and continue to water regularly until it is well established and is making new leafy growth.

In windswept areas and until the tree is established, you may need to provide staking or protection from prevailing winds. Use hessian and canes to make a temporary windbreak for the newly planted trees.

Bay (*Laurus* spp.) is a good tree for a herb garden, because it offers height and can be clipped into attractive shapes or even grown as a standard, with a round lollipop head.

A selection of troughs and tubs

there is scope to use empty pots for special effects.

Herbs grown in containers need special treatment and care, and their maintenance may be more time-consuming than that of plants grown in the garden (see page 159). All containers, including large tubs and troughs, must have drainage holes in their bases, and they should all have a layer of drainage material, such as old crocks and gravel. Use a soil-based compost mixed with water-retentive granules or gel and a slow-release fertilizer. Always water plants in containers regularly during the growing season, even if you have used the water-retentive material.

Troughs and tubs

Troughs and tubs are more substantial than most containers, and they are usually sited where they

In a small garden you can increase the size of your herb collection by growing herbs in containers on several levels. Do not overcrowd the pots and remember that container-grown plants need regular watering.

can be left permanently. Their size makes it possible to plant them up with a number of interesting herbs, and to use them in a decorative way.

Half-barrel or oak tubs are particularly useful for invasive herbs such as mints. A collection of mint, chives and nasturtium planted into a barrel will provide an attractive and useful splash of colour, especially if it is sited near the backdoor.

Large containers need the softening effects of trailing plants, such as nasturtium, ivy and thymes. Arrangements in large troughs and tubs can include smaller pots containing plants such as canary balm (*Cedronella canariensis*) and sage-leaved germander or wood sage (*Teucrium scorodonia*) to provide summer interest. Remove the canary balm in late autumn and overwinter it in a greenhouse, replacing the tender plants with ones that will provide winter interest, including primulas, pansies and violas. Plant the primulas and pansies in autumn, together with the wood violets. In spring, when you tidy up the trough, plant in the nasturtium *Tropaeolum majus* 'Whirlybird Peach Melba', which

It is easy to ring the changes and replace herbs quickly as different varieties become available during the season. If any of the herbs die or you harvest them so completely that they are no longer attractive, it is a simple task to remove and replace them.

If you are going to be using the herbs and replacing them regularly, you can leave them in their individual containers, all set into a sturdy wooden windowbox, with the box becoming a cache-pot for the smaller containers. You can replace any herb that is not growing well without having to replant the whole box.

Herbs for the windowbox

A number of herbs will do well grown together in a container in a sunny situation. Avoid tall-growing plants, not only because most windows open outwards but also because they will always flop over the edge and, in windy weather, may be damaged.

Neat, clump- or mound-forming plants, such as thyme, chives, chervil, parsley, salad burnet and buckler-leaf sorrel, are useful and attractive choices, as are basil, winter savory and marjoram. Rosemary and sage can be grown in a window-box, but they will need less water than the other herbs and because they make woody growth, will soon outgrow their allotted space and lose their decorative charms.

You can combine culinary herbs, such as pot marigold and chives, with more ornamental herbs including nasturtium (whose flowers and leaves are edible in salads). For a permanent framework, grow low-growing junipers and add frost-tender herbs such as basil only when all danger of frost is over.

Planting a windowbox

Before you plant a windowbox, make certain that it is securely fixed in position. Place a layer of broken terracotta shards or stones in the base of the windowbox as a drainage layer, then cover the crocks with a layer of a soil-based potting compost.

Next, remove the herbs from their pots, taking care to avoid root damage. Set them in place in the windowbox. Use a trowel, a small pot or your hands to add compost and to fill in the spaces around each herb. Firm down the compost around each plant and continue to add compost to fill the box to about 2.5cm (1in) below the rim.

Water the herbs in well and cover the surface with a layer of grit to hold the compost in place and to act as a water-absorbent mulch.

Hanging baskets

Hanging baskets, cascading with colourful annuals, are a familiar sight on house fronts, and if you use plants with edible flowers and salad leaves you can create practical as well as attractive arrangements.

A sheltered, sunny site for the hanging basket and careful preparation of the planting medium are the keys to creating a successful and attractive suspended herb garden.

There are several different types of basket to choose from, including half-baskets that hang on hooks close to the wall. As with windowboxes, the security of the fixings, usually wall brackets or hooks, is vital.

It is possible to buy baskets that are on special stands that allow you to raise and lower the basket, so that you can water it effectively without losing compost and wasting water.

Apart from direct regular watering you can provide a reservoir of water for the hanging basket plants by using water-retentive granules. Before you fill the basket, mix the granules or gel into the compost. Water the compost well, and the water-retentive material will hold water, making it available to the plant roots over a longer period.

Prepare the basket for planting by standing it in a bucket. This keeps it balanced while you work around it. First, line it with moss to provide an attractive outer layer. Next, insert a dark plastic liner – black or green plastic looks best. Make a few drainage holes in the plastic, then part fill the basket with the mixture of compost and water-retentive granules.

To protect the delicate roots, wrap absorbent paper around small plants that you want to plant in the sides and base of the basket. Draw them through the moss, and make holes just large enough for them to pass through the plastic liner. Draw them into the basket from the outside, through the moss and liner, so that roots are inside

Planted up in spring, a hanging basket will be a colourful and productive small herb garden for a balcony or patio. It needs careful and frequent watering. Remove spent flowers to keep a succession of colours.

Hanging baskets are often used for summer annuals, but they can look just as attractive – and be useful – when they are planted up with colourful trailing and compact herbs. Remember that hanging baskets need to be watered every day, even if you have included water-retentive granules in the compost.

the basket. Once they are in position you can cut away the paper. Set the other plants into the top of the basket, planting quite closely, then add more compost until it is about 2.5cm (1in) from the rim.

It is best to avoid tall-growing plants, such as lovage, as they will be top-heavy for the basket. Thymes and low-growing herbs, including prostrate rosemary (*Rosmarinus officinalis* Prostratus Group) and winter savory (*Satureja montana*), are useful additions to the basket planting.

For a culinary basket use chives, with thymes to edge the basket and to cover the sides and nasturtiums to tumble over the edge and wind up the chains. Parsley is also useful in a herb basket, as are marjoram and basil, provided the basket is in full sun and out of wind.

Watering is essential for the success of the plantings. Water every day, and in very sunny periods or when there is a drying wind, the baskets may need to be watered as often as three or four times a day. If you have a basket that can be raised and lowered, watering will be easier, and it is also possible to buy a special device for watering hanging baskets to fit to your hosepipe. Never apply a fierce jet of water to hanging baskets, though, as this will probably dislodge compost and may damage the plants.

Deadhead flowering plants such as heartsease, daisies and chives to keep a succession of flowers. If any plants become untidy or fail to thrive, remove them and let the other plants grow to fill their spaces.

Growing herbs indoors

Growing herbs indoors is much more time consuming and labour intensive than keeping them outdoors.

Light is one of the most important factors for the indoor herb collection. When they are growing outdoors, sunlight enables plants to make their own nutrients in their leaves. So the best site for a healthy plant that will produce plenty of leaves and flowers for you to use or enjoy is the sunniest windowsill, where the plants will receive the most light. Because of the lower lights levels indoors, plants are likely to become leggy and tall, so your harvest will be beneficial, as you prune them into bushy and compact shapes.

If you are growing a culinary collection for daily use, rotate the plants so that they develop

Choose a sunny windowsill for your indoor winter herb collection. Sage (*Salvia* spp.), parsley (*Petroselinum* spp.), rosemary (*Rosmarinus* spp.) and bay (*Laurus* spp.) will provide you with material throughout winter, and basil (*Ocimum* spp.) will last until midwinter.

plant cultivation and management

Soil

Before you start to prepare the ground or even to think about what you will plant, you need to know what type of soil you have in your garden. The soil is the most important ingredient you have, and it must be taken care of it, so that you can produce healthy herbs, as well as ornamental plants and vegetables.

There are four main types of soil: sandy, peat, clay or heavy, and loamy. You can often determine the structure of the soil just by looking at it and from its feel. A light, sandy soil, for example, will fall through your fingers, like sand going through an hour-glass, while a heavy clay soil will be sticky and can be moulded into shapes. Neither is suitable for growing plants successfully, but each can be amended to improve the structure. If you fork in organic material to both types of soil, and grit into the clay soil, you will make both kinds easier to work and better for the plants.

Apart from its structure, you need to know whether the soil is acid or alkaline. This is measured on a scale known as the pH scale, which ranges from 1 to 14. Take some samples of soil from different parts of the garden and use a soil test kit to find out what kind of soil you have. These kits are available from garden centres and nurseries, and they are not difficult to use. You need to take samples from various places within your garden because the soil type may vary within quite a small area. If the reading is below 7, the soil is acid or sour; if it is at 7, it is neutral; if it is above 7, it is alkaline. An average garden soil has a pH of between 4.5 and 8.5.

Most herbs prefer soils that are neutral (7) to just slightly alkaline (8.5). If your soil is acid, you may need to raise the pH level by liming the soil annually. You can do this by adding dolomitic limestone. Another more permanent method is to add calcified seaweed, which is available as a liquid and in powdered form. Unlike the limestone, this will not leach out of the soil, and it contains other nutrients that are important for plants.

In general, herbs are undemanding plants that grow well in most garden soils, sites and conditions. In particular, though, they do well on free-draining loam soils with a well-aerated structure. In such soils in winter their roots are less likely to be affected by cold, waterlogged conditions. Sun and shade, dry and moist conditions are more likely to influence the selection of herbs you can grow than the acidity of the soil.

A slightly chalky soil will suit box (*Buxus* spp.), catnip (*Nepeta cataria*), chicory (*Cichorium* spp.), cowslip (*Primula veris*), hyssop (*Hyssopus officinalis*), juniper (*Juniperus* spp.), lily-of-the-valley (*Convallaria majalis*), marjoram (*Origanum* spp.), pinks (*Dianthus* spp.), rosemary (*Rosmarinus* spp.) and salad burnet (*Sanguisorba minor*). If the soil is slightly acid, comfrey (*Symphytum officinale*), foxglove (*Digitalis* spp.), honeysuckle (*Lonicera* spp.), pennyroyal (*Mentha pulegium*), sorrel (*Rumex acetosa*) and sweet cicely (*Myrrhis odorata*) will grow better than average.

Damp conditions suit mints (*Mentha* spp.), so a solution to its rampant nature may be to plant it near the edges of a boggy area around a pond. Chervil (*Anthriscus cerefolium*) and buckler-leaf sorrel (*Rumex scutatus*) are among the few herb plants that prefer shady conditions.

Making a new herb bed

A new herb bed is most likely to be cut from an area of turf, and it will need considerable work before it can be planted up. First of all, if it is to be rectangular or square, mark out the shape of the bed using pegs and strings. If the bed is to have an informal shape, mark the area with sand if the site is already dug, or use a wavy line, such as a hosepipe, to provide you with the outline for elongated, kidney-shaped borders or beds. This is the most flexible way of working, since you can adjust the shape on the ground until you find the one that suits your planting scheme best or is visually attractive to you. Once you are satisfied with the shape, fill a bottle with sand and dribble the sand in a thin line along the string or hosepipe.

If the site is under lawn, begin to dig out the final shape. Use a semi-circular, sharp-bladed edging tool to mark out several rows of turf, then use a sharp-edged spade or turfing spade and slide

Whether you plan to have a large or small herb garden, you need to prepare the ground well to have good results later on.

Dig individual holes for the plants, in already well-prepared, weed-free soil. Make the hole large enough to accommodate the plant's roots when they are spread out. If the plant is slightly pot-bound, you should tease its roots away from the soil or the compost in which they are growing. You can add fertilizer to each planting hole, although if you have already incorporated organic matter into the soil this will not be necessary. Turn the plant upside down in its pot and gently knock it, holding it gently in one hand. Place it in the hole and backfill with soil. Firm it in, then water it in thoroughly. If you are putting in a number of plants, add water to each planting hole individually and then afterwards water the whole area.

After planting, you can nip the growing tips out of shrubby herbs, such as sage and thyme, to encourage them to make a compact bushy shape as they grow.

If you are growing a number of different plants or a single, special herb, you may wish to label them for your records. Put the label in place when you plant. It is all too easy to forget which plant is which when you have planted several in one session. Another way of keeping a record of the plants is to have a special herb garden notebook, with rough sketches of the garden on which you can indicate the positions of individual plants.

Invasive herbs, such as mint or comfrey, should either be relegated to special areas in the garden where they can romp away, or they should be contained in some way to control their natural tendency to spread. An old metal or plastic bucket is the perfect container to sink into the ground to hold mint or comfrey in check.

Herbs in containers

Herbs grown in containers can be treated almost as accessories to the garden scheme. They give you the flexibility to ring the changes and replace them quickly as different varieties become available during the season. If any of the herbs die or you harvest them so much that they are no longer attractive, it is

Grow several different herbs in containers of varying shapes and sizes for a decorative effect. Site them in full sun for best results.

a simple task to remove and replace the herbs.

There are two factors you need to be sure of when planting up a container. First, the optimum depth must be at least 25–30cm (10–12in) to give the roots adequate space to make strong root runs. Second, when it is full of moist soil, a container will be very heavy, so either prepare it *in situ* or, if it is a windowbox, make sure it is securely fixed before you begin to work on it.

Plants in containers need regular watering, since they have available only the water in the soil in the pot. However, because most herbs prefer their roots to be relatively dry, good drainage is essential. The containers must have drainage holes, and when you are planting them up, make sure there is an adequate layer of drainage material such as old pot shards and gravel. Cover the drainage holes with large pieces of crocking to stop compost draining out with the water.

Remove the individual herbs from their pots and place them onto a drainage layer of broken crocks and a layer of soil-based compost. Fill the spaces between the herbs with compost and firm the plants in with your hands. Water the soil and cover the surface with a layer of grit. If you are going to be using the herbs and replacing them regularly, you can leave them in their individual containers, using the container as a cache-pot for several smaller containers. You can replace any herb that is not growing well without having to replant the whole box.

Several herbs will do well growing together in a container in a sunny situation. Neat, clump- or mound-forming plants, including thyme (*Thymus* spp.), chives (*Allium schoenoprasum*), chervil (*Anthriscus cerefolium*), parsley (*Petroselinum crispum*), salad burnet (*Sanguisorba minor*) and buckler-leaf sorrel (*Rumex scutatus*), are useful and attractive choices. Basil (*Ocimum basilicum*), winter savory (*Satureja montana*), marjoram (*Origanum vulgare*) and nasturtium (*Tropaeolum majus*) are ideal choices. Rosemary (*Rosmarinus* spp.) and sage (*Salvia* spp.) can be grown in a windowbox, but they will need less water than the other herbs, and because they make woody growth, will soon outgrow the box.

If you have limited space, think about a high-rise effect and grow your herbs in containers on tiered stands or attached to wall mounts, against a sunny wall.

Discard the middle section, which contains the old, less vigorous part of the plant, and divide the remainder into several pieces which you can replant elsewhere in the garden.

Water in the divisions well and cut back by a half their stems and leaves. Always divide plants in spring or autumn, when the resulting new plants will be able to establish well.

Root cuttings

One of the simplest ways of increasing or propagating the herbs you grow is to take root cuttings in spring or autumn from healthy-looking plants. Mint (*Mentha* spp.), bergamot (*Monarda* spp.), lemon balm (*Melissa officinalis*), horseradish (*Armoracia rusticana*), comfrey (*Symphytum officinale*) and sweet woodruff (*Galium odoratum*) are among the herbs that can be increased in this way.

In the case of mint, which is known for its invasive, creeping rootstock, it is sensible to take root cuttings every few years to provide healthy new plants. Mint is prone to rust, a fungal disease that weakens the plant and makes it unattractive in the herb garden and unpleasant to use in cooking or as a garnish. So when you take root cuttings from mint, make sure you take them from healthy plants that have none of the rusty coloured spots that are the symptoms of the disease. If any of your mint plants shows signs of rust, cut out and burn the affected parts, and if the plant is badly affected, dig it out completely and discard it.

Forcing mint for winter leaves

You can also dig up a clump of mint roots and pot them up to provide you with a fresh supply of this versatile aromatic herb throughout winter. Mint is a herbaceous perennial, which dies down in the winter, losing its above-ground stems and leaves. If you pot the roots up in autumn and keep them in a light, warm place for a few weeks, you can force it into new growth. A warm greenhouse or a sunny windowsill indoors are ideal situations for forcing mint.

After a few weeks, when leafy shoots show above the soil surface, water the plant. When the shoots are about 10cm (4in) high, nip out the growing points to encourage the development of sideshoots. Keep the potted mint in a warm, light position indoors or in the greenhouse through the winter, and enjoy its leaves in sauces or in salads and marinades.

Rooting horseradish

Horseradish (*Armoracia rusticana*), with its piquant flavoured root, reproduces so easily from root cuttings that it can be a menace in the herb garden. However, if you enjoy the sauce that can be made from its pungent roots, you will need sufficient plants to provide a constant supply. It is an invasive plant and will spread naturally to make a large clump. It will grow a new plant from the smallest piece of root, so that if you dig it up and a piece of root breaks off, you can be sure that a new plant will grow from the broken rootstock.

If you want to increase your stock of horse radish in a more orderly way, take several root cuttings from one piece of root in spring. Pot them up to start them off and transplant them into their growing site the following spring.

Year-round maintenance

Throughout the year in the herb garden there are seasonal tasks that keep the plants healthy, provide you with extra or new plants, maintain the look of the garden and provide you with one of the most pleasant harvests a garden can offer: fragrant and useful leaves, flowers and seeds. Part of the seasonal activity in a herb garden takes place out of it, when you use the produce harvested from it in cooking, for making aromatic gifts and in the planning of the next year's seeds and designs.

Herbs in the garden are generally trouble free and will grow well without a great deal of maintenance. The schedule outlined here will ensure that the garden looks at its best all year round.

Watering and weeding

In a dry spring or summer keep nursery beds watered and make sure that all herbs growing in containers are regularly watered. You should water herbs in containers in the greenhouse as often as necessary.

In the herb garden, cut back stems that have carried flowers to encourage a second flush of foliage. Harvest flowers and seedheads to dry.

Harvesting

Harvesting herbs is one of the most pleasurable tasks in the herb garden, and this is a time when you will be able to appreciate to the full all the aromatic properties of the plants. Coincidentally, harvesting is a certain method of encouraging the plants to develop into attractive, bushy shapes, and it also promotes the production of the leafy shoots you need for kitchen, cosmetic or aromatic purposes indoors.

Evergreen herbs, including thyme, sage, rosemary and bay, can be harvested from outdoor and indoor herb collections all year round, as can herbs that you have forced into growth in winter, such as mint, tarragon and chives. Annual herbs, including perilla, rocket, dill, nasturtium and coriander, are at their best in spring and summer, while basil reaches it peak in late summer.

Herbaceous perennial herbs, including fennel, lovage and comfrey, die back in winter, so their leaves are available for harvest only during the growing season. Wait until they are growing well and there is enough leafy material available before you begin to harvest from them. Cut from each plant evenly, so that you retain the overall decorative shape of each plant. Over-cutting will result in stunted, unattractive growth, and if you remove all the leaves, you remove the plant's means of making its own food and it will weaken and die.

When to harvest

For a handful of leaves to add to salads or cooking, pick the herbs just before you want to use them at any time of the day. If you need a large quantity of herbs to preserve in oils, vinegars or sugars, or if you want to dry, freeze or microwave herbs, pick them early, on a dry, warm day, before it gets hot and the aromatic oils in the leaves evaporate in the sun's heat.

How to harvest

Cleanliness and speed are the crucial factors. Use sharp, clean scissors or a sharp, clean kitchen knife to harvest herbs. Sometimes you can break off stems from woody plants, such as sage and thyme, but it is best to cut what you need from the plant, without damaging the delicate leaves. Work quickly and keep the harvested herbs in a cool place or in a trug, flat wooden box or tray lined with damp paper or moist kitchen towels to protect them from damage. Herbs that you are harvesting for their foliage, are at their best before the plant comes into flower, so as part of your regular herb garden maintenance nip out the growing tips of plants to keep leaf production going.

Only harvest as much as you can process in one session quickly and easily, before the plants wilt and lose their usefulness. The foliage of herbs such as basil will become limp very quickly, so it should be dried, frozen or microwaved as soon as possible after harvesting to preserve the flavours adequately. The water content of herbs is over 70 per cent, and once this is lost, they lose colour and flavour rapidly.

Harvesting herb flowers

Many herbs are grown for their attractive and edible flowers as well as for their foliage. Nasturtiums, chives, borage, pot marigold, salad burnet and basil are just a few herbs whose flowers can be used to add sparkle and flavour to salads and drinks.

Use sharp scissors to snip them off the stems when they are in bud or just beginning to open up. Handle them gently so that they are not damaged or bruised. If you plan to use the flowers for dried arrangements, pick them with long stems and dry them tied into bunches.

Harvest flowers as you would foliage, by picking early in the day. As you harvest, lay the flowers into a trug or basket lined with moistened sheets of kitchen towel. Try to keep the basket in the shade as you work and only harvest flowers that are in perfect condition. Pick rosebuds just as they begin to open to dry for pot pourri.

Many herbs, such as rosemary, sage and lavender, can be air dried in a relatively short time. Remove foliage from the flower stems of lavender and, in general, tie herbs into bunches of between ten and twenty stems. Hang them upside from hooks, or peg them to a wire hanger. Dry them in a warm, dry, well-ventilated room.

plant directory

bright room indoors, potting them on into containers with a nutrient-rich, loam-based compost. Pinch out growing tips of plants to encourage bushy growth. Pick and air-dry the lemon-scented leaves for use in pot pourri.

Many other species of eucalyptus are useful in commercial medicinal preparations, and some, like cider gum (*E. gunnii*), are very decorative.

Eupatorium
Joe Pye weed or gravelroot (*Eupatorium purpureum*), a hardy herbaceous perennial, is a good border plant. The erect stems, which can grow to 1.8m (6ft), need no staking. The large, oval and aromatic leaves are green with purplish markings in the veins, and the plant has clusters of pink flowerheads, which open to a pinkish-cream in summer. Sow seed into a sunny or partially shaded position. Joe Pye weed prefers a moist, well-drained soil. Cut back after flowering and divide large groups in autumn.

Traditionally used medicinally and as a dye plant, today Joe Pye weed holds its place in the herb garden, as well as in the ornamental garden, for its attractive flowers and usefulness as a tall border plant.

Boneset (*E. perfoliatum*) grows to 1.5m (5ft) and has similar flowers to Joe Pye weed, except they are white. Also attractive is hemp agrimony (*E. cannabinum*), which is slightly lower growing – to 1.2m (4ft) – and has mauve to pink flowers.

Filipendula
With its creamy-white, downy-soft looking flowers, meadowsweet (*Filipendula ulmaria*) does well in a shady, moist and fertile soil. It is a hardy herbaceous perennial, whose fragrant flowers were used as flavourings for beer and mead. It has a long association as a medicinal herb and was once used as a strewing herb to perfume homes. There are golden-leaved, variegated and double-flowered forms.

Foeniculum
A hardy perennial, with finely cut aromatic leaves and umbels of small yellow flowers in summer, fennel (*Foeniculum vulgare*) grows to 2.1m (7ft). In spring its leaves are particularly attractive as they unfurl from pale green leaf sheaths. Grow it in a sunny site in well-drained, rich soil, sowing seed direct into the growing site or into pots in a green-house for earlier germination. Either thin or transplant to a spacing of 50cm (20in). Pick leaves as needed through the summer and the seed in autumn, when it is ripe. Divide established plants in spring or autumn. The leaves are a flavour-some addition to salads and soups and they make a good garnish. Fennel is also often used in fish dishes, while the seeds are used in cooking and to make teas or tisanes.

Bronze fennel (*F. v.* 'Purpureum') has chocolate-brown, feathery leaves, which contrast well with the green of ordinary fennel. Florence fennel (*F. v.* var. *dulce*) is grown as an annual for its swollen leaf base or bulb. Sow seed of Florence fennel in late spring and harvest the bulbs, for use in salads or as cooked vegetables, in autumn.

Galium
A hardy perennial, sweet woodruff (*Galium odoratum*; syn. *Asperula odorata*) is a shady woodland, ground-covering plant, growing to 30cm (12in). It produces delicate, ruff-like leaves and small white flowers in spring. Sow seed in late summer into trays and keep in a cold frame over winter. Plant out when well established in late spring. Grow it in partial shade in a moist, well-drained soil. Water young plants in well and make sure they do not dry out in dry weather. Pick leaves through the summer and dry them to allow the characteristic smell of freshly mown hay to develop. Pick flowers as they open and dry them to include in pot pourri and use the leaves in sachets as moth repellents.

Lady's bedstraw (*G. verum*) is a yellow-flowered perennial. Grow it in a shady site in a moist but well-drained soil. The sweet-scented flowers were once used for strewing, and the whole plant has medicinal uses. The foliage provides a yellow dye, which is used as a colouring for cheese and butter.

Hamamelis
In late winter or early spring Virginian witch hazel (*Hamamelis virginiana*) produces a fizz of fire-cracker-bright flowers on bare grey stems. The deciduous leaves appear in late spring, and they also provide good autumnal colour. Witch hazel grows as a shrub or a small tree and can reach 5m (over 16ft). It does best in sun or semi-shade in an enriched, damp, neutral to acid soil. Propagate by layering or taking cuttings in spring.

Harvest leaves in summer to make ointments; commercially, the leaves are the source of cooling, astringent witch hazel.

Chinese witch hazel (*H. mollis*) has similar flowers and growth habit to Virginian witch hazel. The flowers are very fragrant, making it a good choice for an evening arbour or other aromatic design.

Helianthus
A tall-growing annual, common sunflower (*Helianthus annuus*) was prized as an economic crop for its seeds, which were used to make flour and other foodstuffs. Oil was produced from the seeds as early as the eighteenth century.

There are numerous species and cultivars within the genus, of varying height, shape and flower colour, but they all bring colour and interest to the ornamental herb garden. Grow them in full sun in a well-drained soil.

H. a. 'Teddy Bear' is a low-growing form with a shaggy flowerhead of fully double ray florets. Other useful cultivars include the richly coloured Music Box Mixed Series. Another species of *Helianthus*,

Jerusalem artichoke (*H. tuberosus*), has yellow flowers and produces edible roots.

Helichrysum
A small, frost hardy, perennial subshrub, curry plant (*Helichrysum italicum*; syn. *H. angustifolium*) has very pungent aromatic, silver, strap-like leaves and carries small bobbles of yellow flowers in summer. Grow it in well-drained, rich soil and cut back to keep a good shape in early autumn or winter. Remove flowering tops when the flowers are spent. Pick flowers to dry in summer, when they are just opening. The leaves can be harvested at any time. Buy new plants if required in spring to replace any that have been damaged by frost. *H. i.* 'Nanum' is a dwarf form that grows to 25cm (10cm).

Grow curry plant as a grey 'ribbon' in a formal knot garden or as an edging plant, but only if you enjoy its strong aromas. Use flowers to add colour to pot pourri.

Hemerocallis
An ornamental, lily-like perennial, which will form large clumps, the day lily (*Hemerocallis* spp.) is an attractive plant for cottage gardens and is an asset in the edible flower garden. It grows well in full sun, in a moist, enriched and well-drained soil. The opulent flowers open for just a day. Pick the buds just as they form and the flowers as they open to use fresh, or dry for later use. They are tradition-ally used in Asian and Chinese cuisine and are nutritious and vitamin-rich.

There are numerous species and hybrids to grow for their ornamental qualities, as well as for their taste, including *H. fulva*, a semi-evergreen species with attractive dark green foliage and profuse yellow-orange, trumpet-like flowers.

Hesperis
A hardy biennial, sweet rocket (*Hesperis matronalis*) makes a plump, leafy rosette in its first season, followed by tall, stately spires that carry fists of mauve or white flowers, depending on the form. It is sweetly scented and is a favourite cottage garden plant. Grow it in rich, moist, but well-drained soil, in sun or partial shade. It is a useful for a mixed border and for fragrance in a perfumed arbour.

H. m. var. *albiflora* is a white-flowered form.

Humulus
When it is growing well, hop (*Humulus lupulus*), a vigorous, hardy climbing plant, reaches 7m (23ft) in a season. It is a perennial and dies down in winter, but in spring its rough stems, with fresh green, toothed and roughly heart-shaped leaves, begin to twine around willing and unwilling supports. Make sure you plant it where you want it to grow, or you will be forever fighting it. In late summer female plants bear papery, yellowish-green, cone-shaped flower-heads. It needs full sun in fertile, deeply dug soil, and you must plant hops against a fence, trellis or strong support. Divide and replant rooted stems in spring and take cuttings in early summer.

Use young shoots or 'hop tops' in spring and leaves in summer to cook or make infusions. Leaves are boiled to make a dye, and the stems can be woven into baskets or used for herbal wreaths. The aromatic flowers were once widely used in beer making, but today they are more likely to be dried and placed in small pillows to aid sleep.

H. l. 'Aureus' has sulphur green, almost golden leaves and makes a good display against a background of evergreen shrubs.

Hyssopus
A small evergreen shrub, with thin, aromatic leaves and spikes of blue, pink or white flowers in late summer, hyssop (*Hyssopus officinalis*) grows to 1m (over 3ft). Grow it in full sun in light, well-drained alkaline soil. Sow seed in spring to 60cm (24in) apart. Divide roots in spring or take stem cuttings from spring to autumn. Cut back after flowering and also if it is being grown as an informal hedge plant, for which it is ideal. If it is clipped severely, hyssop can also be used in more formal knot gardens. Pick flowers to use as garnishes in salads or in herb posies as needed, and in early summer pick foliage stems to dry for use in sleep pillows. It also has medicinal uses.

H. o. subsp. *aristatus* is a low-growing, compact plant with purple flowers and narrow leaves. *H. o.* f. *roseus* is a soft pink-flowered form, while *H. o.* f. *albus* is the white-flowered form.

Inula
Elecampane (*Inula helenium*) is a hardy herbaceous perennial, with yellow, daisy-like flowers and long, pointed leaves. It can grow to a height of 1.5m (5ft) and more. Sow seeds in spring into a sunny position in rich, moist soil. Keep well watered and weed free until established. Divide plants in spring or autumn. Elecampane has long been used as a medicinal plant, and it was grown in monastery gardens. The roots can be harvested and sliced into rounds then dried for use in pot pourri.

I. orientalis (syn. *I. glandulosa*) has orange-yellow flowers and grows to 90cm (36in), while *I. magnifica* is similar in appearance to elecampane but has much larger flowerheads.

Iris
Orris (*Iris germanica* var. *florentina*), which grows from a rhizome, is a perennial that bears large, greyish-white, typical iris-like flowers in early summer. The broad, sword-shaped leaves grow in a fan arrangement from the rhizome to a height of 60cm (24in). Plant rhizomes in spring or early autumn, leaving the top of the rhizome exposed so that it can bake in the sun. Plant in full sun or partial shade in free-draining, neutral soil. Divide every three or four years, replanting the younger, outer portions.

For more ornamental effect, use

I. 'Blue Shimmer', which bears its attractively coloured flowers over a long period, while yellow flag (*I. pseudacorus*) is useful in the wild flower garden.

Use second- and third-year growth of orris to dry as orris root for pot pourri. Grind and store for two years to allow the powder to mature before it is used.

Jasminum

Common jasmine or jessamine (*Jasminum officinale*) is a hardy, deciduous climber with delicate ferny leaves and fragrant, pink-tinged white, trumpet-shaped flowers in summer and autumn. Take semi-ripe cuttings in summer, and when they are well-rooted plant them out in open, well-drained, fertile soil, in a sheltered but sunny position.

Harvest flowers as they open to dry for use in pot pourri or jasmine tea.

Juniperus

There are upright and prostrate forms of common juniper (*Juniperus communis*), an attractive and aromatic conifer. It grows to 4m (over 13ft) or more, depending on variety and form, and it will grow well in average garden soil in sun or shade. Although it is grown commercially for its small, blue, aromatic fruits, they take several years to ripen from green to a purple with a deep bloom on the skin. In the herb garden it is more often grown for its ornamental value and for its medicinal associations.

Use the upright form *J. c.* 'Hibernica' for an erect, architectural shape. Prostrate varieties, such as *J. c.* 'Green Carpet', are useful as ground cover in a foliage planting.

Laurus

Bay laurel or sweet bay (*Laurus nobilis*) is an evergreen tree with shiny, aromatic and spicy leaves, small yellow flowers and black berries. It will grow to 15m (almost 50ft), but in most gardens it is slow growing, and when it is grown in containers

its height is restricted. Grow it in full sun if possible, although it will tolerate light shade. It grows best in a rich, well-drained soil. Protect young plants and plants in containers from frost with straw bales and hessian windbreaks. Cut back any frost-damaged stems in spring. Take stem cuttings in spring.

Pick leaves as required throughout the year. Bay is traditionally part of the classic *bouquet garni,* and it is used in many savoury dishes. It is also a good flavouring for sweet rice puddings and other milk desserts. Always simmer the milk gently with the bay leaf before adding the other ingredients. Bay is also used medicinally.

L. n. 'Aurea' has golden leaves and makes an attractive colour contrast in the herb garden, but it may need protection in winter until it is well established. The willowleaf bay (*L. n.* f. *angustifolia*) is also attractive as a container plant and in the garden.

Lavandula

With their grey-green, softly textured, highly aromatic leaves and fragrant deep blue, purple, white or pink flowers, the various species and varieties of lavender (*Lavandula* spp.) are among the most popular of all garden plants. Lavender is an evergreen shrub, which can grow to 1m (over 3ft). The aromatic leaves and bee-attracting flowers are among its charms for herb growers. It does best in a sunny, open site in well-drained, slightly sandy soil. Cut back any woody stems in autumn and remove any spent flowerheads left on the plant from the previous season's flowering. Gather flowers for drying as they open. Sow fresh seed in late summer or autumn, and transplant seedlings to 60cm (24in) apart in the border or to 30cm (12in) if it is being grown as a hedge. You can also take cuttings in summer.

In the garden lavender is useful as an edging or hedging plant, but the range of heights that is available makes it also suitable for different

positions in a mixed border. The overall uniformity of shape and colour that can be achieved by using plants of the same species or variety make it useful in formal as well as informal situations. The flowers can be used for culinary purposes and are attractive in arrangements if dried. Lavender has traditional uses in medicine and aromatherapy, in cosmetic and perfume production.

There are many species and varieties to choose from, but probably the most popular is *L. angustifolia* 'Hidcote' which has a very uniform, compact shape and produces deep blue flowers. Other common cultivars of *L. angustifolia*, such as 'Imperial Gem' (deep purple, fragrant flowers), 'Miss Katherine' (deep pink flowers) and 'Royal Purple' (good for drying), and the hybrid *L.* × *intermedia* 'Grappenhall', are also decorative and aromatic choices. Some lavenders, including French lavender (*L. stoechas*) and woolly lavender (*L. lanata*), are less hardy and will need winter protection.

Your choice from this wonderful genus or aromatic herb garden favourites will be governed by local availability, although many nurseries do sell unusual lavenders by mail order.

Leonurus

Chinese motherwort (*Leonurus sibiricus*) is a biennial, which produces leaves in its first year and flowers in the second year. It has attractive, deeply cut and emphatically marked or veined leaves. The flowers, which appear in late summer of the second year, are small, pinky-white and lipped. They are followed by black nutlets or seedpods. Grow Chinese motherwort in moist but well-drained soil in sun or partial shade. Sow seed in spring or buy new plants every second year.

Chinese motherwort has a long history in traditional Chinese medicine, but in modern herb gardens it is prized for its distinctive foliage.

Levisticum

A hardy perennial, growing to 2m (over 6ft), lovage (*Levisticum officinale*) has large, dark green leaves and clusters of small, pale ochre flowers in late summer. It does best in a sunny site in rich, well-drained soil. Seed should be sown in late summer. Water plants until they are well established, and divide them every two or three years, in autumn or spring.

Lovage's height makes it useful as a tall accent plant at the centre of a kitchen herb garden. It also looks attractive near angelica (*Angelica archangelica*), and if it is grown at the base of a rose, it will hide the rose's bare stems. Pick leaves as and when they are needed, and harvest seeds when they are ripe. Fresh leaves and stalks are used to add a distinctive, celery-like flavour to soups and stews, and young leaves may be used in salads and as a garnish for savoury dishes.

Lilium

Stately and fragrant, the madonna lily (*Lilium candidum*) has a long association in both herb and cottage gardens, where the flowers are enjoyed for their overwhelming fragrance. Grow the bulbs in full sun in a neutral to alkaline soil. Madonna lily bulbs should be just covered with soil, because they need to be baked in the sun if they are to do themselves justice. Propagate from seed in autumn or spring, or from offsets produced by the bulbs in late summer.

Both the regal lily (*L. regale*) and the martagon or Turk's cap lily (*L. martagon*) and its white-flowered form, *L. m.* var. *album*, are also favourites in the herb garden. *L.* 'Star Gazer' is a colourful, late-flowering and scented modern lily that is popular too.

Lonicera

The twining and climbing habit and scented flowers of honeysuckle (*Lonicera* spp.) offer interesting characteristics for the modern herb garden, and although the plants have medicinal attributes, it is Japanese honeysuckle (*L. japonica*) that continues to be used in Chinese medicine. Grow honeysuckle in well-drained soil in sun or shade and cut it back if necessary after flowering. You can grow it over upturned hanging baskets to create a topiarized shape.

Italian honeysuckle (*L. caprifolium*) is grown for its fragrant pink to yellow flowers. Japanese honeysuckle (*L. japonica*) has sweetly scented, creamy-yellow, trumpet-shaped flowers. The variety *L. j.* 'Halliana' is particularly vigorous and has white flowers, which turn yellow as they mature. The fragrance of common honeysuckle or woodbine (*L. periclymenum*) hangs in the air, especially in the evening. The yellow to white flowers, flushed with red, are followed by red fruits.

Melissa

Lemon balm or bee balm (*Melissa officinalis*) is a hardy perennial, which grows to 1m (over 3ft) when in flower, with attractive green or variegated lemon-scented foliage through the summer. The plant's soft, mounded shape makes it especially suitable for soft foliage plantings in the front of the border or in the specialist herb garden. It flowers from midsummer to autumn, with untidy spikes of small flowers. Grow lemon balm in partial shade in a well-drained but moist soil. Sow seed in spring and divide established plants in autumn or spring. Cut back flowering stems in late autumn. Pick leaves when required to use fresh and to dry or freeze. Harvest before the plant comes into flower, when the essential oils will be at their strongest.

Lemon balm makes a zesty addition to salads. A few leaves in boiled water make a tasty tea and it also has medicinal uses.

The lemon-yellow variegated form (*M. o.* 'Aurea'; syn. *M. o.* 'Variegata') combines especially well in foliage plantings, but the flower stems should be cut off to encourage leaf production. Once the flowers form, the yellow variegation tends to deteriorate. *M. o.* 'All Gold' is a new and very good form of golden lemon balm. It needs a light position but will scorch in hot sun, so partial shade suits it best.

Mentha

A tough and invasive hardy perennial with a creeping root, mint (*Mentha* spp.) has strongly aromatic leaves with mauve flower spikes in summer. It does best in a moist site in shade but will grow almost anywhere. As mint is so invasive, plant it in a container or confine its roots in an old bucket sunk into the ground. Take root cuttings or divide plants in spring or autumn. A slip will root quickly in water. Mint can be forced into leaf in warm conditions in a greenhouse over winter.

Pick leaves when required and before flowering for the best flavour fresh and later, when dried. Traditionally associated with roast lamb, in the form of mint sauce, it has many other delicious uses, including flavouring new peas and new potatoes, in sweet dishes as a syrup or, as a garnish, with strawberries. It is also good with chocolate and as a flavouring in ice cream and sweets.

Different mints have different flavours and uses, and because of the range of variegation in mint leaves and attractive flowers, it is versatile in the garden. Moroccan spearmint (*M. spicata* 'Moroccan') is used as a tea or tisane. Creeping pennyroyal (*M. pulegium*), which has bright green leaves, is used as an insect repellent to deter ants and fleas. Applemint (*M. suaveolens*) has an apple flavour; its furry leaves have given it a second common name, woolly mint. Also attractive in salads is variegated apple mint or pineapple mint (*M. suaveolens* 'Variegata').

Peppermint (*M.* × *piperita*) has a